# Environmental Disasters, Natural Recovery and Human Responses

Natural disasters destroy more property and kill more people with each passing year. Volcanic eruptions, earthquakes, hurricanes, tsunamis, floods, landslides, fires and other natural events are becoming more frequent and their consequences more devastating. Del Moral and Walker provide a comprehensive summary of the diverse ways in which natural disasters disrupt humanity and how humans cope. Burgeoning human numbers, shrinking resources and intensification of the consequences of natural disasters have produced a crisis of unparalleled proportions. Through this detailed study, the authors provide a template for improving restoration to show how relatively simple approaches can enhance both human well-being and that of the other species on the planet. This book will appeal to ecologists and land managers, as well as anyone curious about the natural world and natural disasters.

ROGER DEL MORAL is Professor of Biology at the University of Washington. His research includes the mechanisms of vegetation response to disturbances caused by volcanoes, glaciers, grazing and urbanization. He has practiced wetland restoration for over 20 years and has experience with dune and subalpine meadow restoration. He has studied volcanoes on four continents, including detailed studies of Mount St. Helens that started in 1980.

LAWRENCE R. WALKER is Professor of Biology at the University of Nevada, Las Vegas. His research focuses on ecological plant succession and the theoretical and practical lessons for restoration. His research in succession and restoration has encompassed work on volcanoes, dunes, glacial moraines, floodplains, landslides, cliffs, hurricanes, reservoir drawdown zones, abandoned roads and mine tailings.

# Environmental Disasters, Natural Recovery and Human Responses

ROGER DEL MORAL
*University of Washington, Seattle*

LAWRENCE R. WALKER
*University of Nevada, Las Vegas*

CAMBRIDGE
UNIVERSITY PRESS

CAMBRIDGE UNIVERSITY PRESS
Cambridge, New York, Melbourne, Madrid, Cape Town, Singapore, São Paulo

Cambridge University Press
The Edinburg Building, Cambridge CB2 8RU, UK

Published in the United States of America by
Cambridge University Press, New York

www.cambridge.org
Information on this title: www.cambridge.org/9780521860345

First published 2007

Printed in the United Kingdom at the University Press, Cambridge

*A catalogue record for this publication is available from the British Library*

*Library of Congress Cataloging in Publication data*
del Moral, Roger, 1943-
    Environmental disasters, natural recovery, and human responses / authors,
Roger del Moral and Lawrence R. Walker.
    p. cm.
    Includes bibliographical references and index.
    ISBN 0-521-86034-2 (hardback) -- ISBN 0-521-67766-1 (pbk.)
    1.   Natural disasters--Environmental aspects.  2.   Ecological disturbances.
    3.   Restoration ecology.   I. Walker, Lawrence R. II. Title.

    QH545.N3M67 2007
    363.34--dc22                                                    2006036332

    ISBN-13   978-0-521-86034-5   hardback
    ISBN-13   978-0-521-67766-0   paperback

# Contents

# Preface and acknowledgements

Each day we are bombarded with news of natural disturbances. Volcanoes rain unimaginable destruction down on mountain villages, hurricanes and tsunamis ravage coastal communities and fires turn lush forests into ashen specters. Such violent events are fundamental, unavoidable parts of the global environment that in the long term restore and rejuvenate the landscape. In the short term, societies must respond to mitigate the devastation.

Human societies are also assailed by silent disturbances that rarely merit mention in the media. Dunes creep out of a desert to swallow an oasis. Exotic species of shrubs invade grazing land. Lake levels slowly fall, eliminating unique biota and cultures. As our numbers increase, humans have unavoidably become a new form of disturbance. We rival volcanoes, floods, dunes and glaciers in the intensity of our impacts. Our actions magnify other disturbances. Grazing gradually turns steppes to deserts and agriculture impoverishes the land. Our industries pollute in both subtle and more blatant ways that merely reduce productivity or poison ecosystems.

Unlike most natural disturbances, human impacts continue to intensify and become more widespread. Worse, as populations burgeon into ever more sensitive habitats, the effects of natural disasters are becoming increasingly devastating.

We are both academic plant ecologists who have spent most of our careers studying ecosystems damaged by nature and by man. We worry greatly that the natural world is shrinking, losing its ability to sustain biodiversity and, indeed, the human species. This book was born of our desire to translate the many lessons biologists have learned by studying natural recovery processes following disasters. We know that this knowledge has direct, practical value for improving the landscapes that support us.

While humans increasingly inflict disasters upon the environment and upon themselves, this book is focused on natural disturbances — events that cause loss of plant and animal life across landscapes — and how humanity interacts to intensify both these events and their effects. We will, however, discuss how human actions can create severe, often novel, disturbances. Many of these new disturbances create surfaces analogous to natural disturbances (pavement resembles lava, for example), but other surfaces are new (toxic mine wastes, heavy metal depositions). Rather than presenting a hand-wringing litany of disasters, we apply lessons gleaned from nature to the restoration of landscapes damaged by both natural and human-created disasters. We will describe many of nature's most dramatic forces that initiate what ecologists call *primary succession*. In addition, we will explore how ecosystems recover from less intense forces in a process called *secondary succession*. The recovery process requires several mechanisms that permit a series of species to establish on newly formed land, often against severe odds. Landscapes not managed by humans will normally recover and, eventually, reconstitute a functioning ecosystem. An understanding of how this happens and what limits the degree and rate of recovery is the foundation of *restoration ecology*. Restoration ecologists seek to redress both natural and anthropogenic destruction of ecosystems. They employ both biological and engineering tools. An understanding of successional processes and the limits of the biota to develop under hostile conditions guide their efforts.

During the last century, humans became more aware of the expanding threats to the environment and to the health of individuals and societies. The insightful writings of scientists such as Edward O. Wilson and Steven J. Gould, humanists such as Wendell Berry and Bill McKibben and economists such as Lester Brown have together addressed these many problems and guided us toward solutions. Our goal is more humble. We seek to demonstrate the awesome powers of disturbances and the splendor of the recuperative powers of the biota. We will demonstrate how natural processes can form the basis for the restoration of sites damaged or destroyed by humans.

In a rapidly changing world, there are severe constraints on effective ecosystem recovery. Exact re-creation of a damaged ecosystem is now recognized as very unlikely. Introduced species are ubiquitous and they can strongly inhibit restoration efforts, particularly if they establish before restoration efforts begin. Modern disturbances are often either more intense or so different from natural counterparts that natural recovery is unlikely. Copper smelters spew metallic fogs that create extensive toxic wastelands which are far more difficult for organisms to colonize than, for example, lava or sand dunes. Most plants have had little evolutionary experience of adapting to heavy metals, so it is manifestly clear that restoration of such landscapes requires intensive, creative effort. Unfortunately, the lack of money often increases the chances that recovery in the aftermath of such disasters will be neither swift nor effective.

In this book, we will demonstrate the lessons natural systems have to teach us about coping with human-inflicted disasters, including how to most efficiently conduct restoration efforts. We will compare the large variety of natural disturbances and recovery and the smaller variety of their human analogues, thereby demonstrating that we can improve our long-term responses to disasters. The restoration of any given landscape requires the recognition that the landscape is damaged, the will to address the problem, and the tools to effect a rational solution. We will establish that there is a critical need for restoration in many circumstances and thus foster and nourish the will to act. We will reveal that by using a natural model with attainable goals, the tools are both available and practical. The time for effective action is now.

The present volume is a summary of natural succession processes that can be applied in order to significantly improve restoration. We wish to show that applying ecological perspectives to restoration can foster a more secure world with fewer limits on human potential. Any failure to accelerate the return of destroyed lands to productivity will only make existing problems worse.

Roger thanks his wife, Beth Brosseau, for making it all work, and Boomer for his faithful companionship. Roger was supported by US NSF grant DEB-0087040, which supported his work on Mount St. Helens and assisted with travel expenses in Iceland, Russia and Italy. The NSF has supported his work on Mount St. Helens since 1980, for which he is grateful.

Lawrence thanks his wife, Elizabeth Powell, for encouraging him by her example to make his work on succession more relevant to practical restoration problems, and his sister Liz Walker and son Simon Baker for demonstrating that careers can be dedicated to reducing human impacts on the environment. Lawrence was supported by a sabbatical leave from the University of Nevada, Las Vegas, by Landcare Research in Lincoln, New Zealand and by US NSF grants DEB-0080538 and DEB-0218039 to the Puerto Rico Long-Term Ecological Research Program.

We both thank the following people for reviews of one or more chapters; Patra V. Alatsis, Nick Brokaw, James Dalling, Chad J. Jones, Dan Kunkle, James Luken, Thomas Marler, Jennifer Ruesink, Alan Walker, Joe Walker and Margery Walker.

The publisher has used its best endeavors to ensure the URLs for external websites referred to in this book are correct at the time of going to press. However, the publisher has no responsibility for the websites and can make no guarantee that a site will remain active or that the content is or will remain appropriate.

# 1

# Introduction: a crescendo of destruction

## 1.1 DISTURBANCE AND HUMAN INTERACTIONS

The pristine world of the past was filled with cataclysms. Volcanoes, earthquakes, floods and fires shaped today's landscapes and every living organism evolved in response to natural disturbance. What we call *Nature* survived in a finely tuned balancing act between the forces of destruction and recovery. Recovery of Nature after destruction was inevitable, but it occurred at variable rates and with a constantly evolving mix of plants and animals. Occasionally natural disturbances were so violent that many species became extinct. Today, the rules have changed; humans have profoundly altered the balance of destruction and recovery, by intensifying natural disturbances and creating many novel ones, without an equal emphasis on recovery. What are the consequences of this meddling by humans with the future of this planet?

Humans have always been at the mercy of large natural disturbances, though we try to forget this fact. The Minoans left little but legends (e.g. Atlantis) after the massive eruption of Santorini (Thera) in about 1623 BC. Agriculture in Japan suffered terrible blows from sixth century volcanic eruptions, as did the economies of both Iceland and Europe by the eruptions of Laki in 1783. Yet we continue to build on active volcanoes, steep slopes prone to erosion and floodplains subject to flooding. Recently, we have felt a growing, yet false, sense of protection from the natural forces of destruction because many of us now live in safe, artificially created environments. Ironically, this decoupling from reality, combined with our immense population growth, results in three dilemmas.

First, that there are many more humans now than ever before implies greater contact with and greater mortality from the same set of natural disturbances. Dense populations now inhabit clusters of cities

Fig. 1.1 The alien butterfly bush (*Buddleja davidii*) is shown in a
New Zealand riverbed. A native of Asia, it has invaded floodplains in
many parts of the world.

where volcanoes once spewed ash onto uninhabited lands. Second, our
collective "ecological footprint" magnifies the effects of natural
disturbances on humans. Tsunamis and hurricanes are more devastating where protective coral reefs and mangrove swamps have been
destroyed. Landslides are more frequent where logging or road building
destabilizes slopes. Deforestation also intensifies the severity of natural
floods, while grazing semi-arid lands fuels the expansion of desert
dunes. Finally, humans continue to modify the earth so much that an
entirely new set of disturbances threatens. These new effects include
pollution, biological invasions (Fig. 1.1), overgrazing (Plate 1) and rapid
global climate change. Mining and energy production create toxic
landscapes (Fig. 1.2). We have homogenized the world's fauna and flora
and global warming is changing how species are distributed around the
world. What was once "background noise" from human activities has
become the principal signal, impossible to ignore.

This book describes how we can harness the natural processes
of recovery to address some of these dilemmas caused by humans.

Fig. 1.2  Coal mine tailings in the Midlands of England (UK) produce extremely acid surfaces that challenge restoration. Many such industrial activities create barren, infertile and toxic environments.

Our challenge is to mitigate the immediate effects of disturbances, then to apply the best knowledge and technology to redress the damage.

There is a synergistic interplay between nature and human actions as humanity expands. The geographic and cultural landscapes of this planet have changed dramatically, altering the interactions among humans and disturbances. As the human population grows, it expands into increasingly fragile environments, intensifying impacts of natural disturbances (Fig. 1.3). With some validity, many natural philosophers speak of the "end of nature", implying that no place on earth now escapes significant human impacts. Against the background of pervasive human impacts, we believe that our efforts to hasten recovery of landscapes should intensify dramatically.

The barrage of recent natural disasters around the world highlights our vulnerability to the forces of Nature. The Indian Ocean tsunami of December 26, 2004 demonstrated that the 39 percent of us living near coastlines are certainly living in a risky habitat. Those not in coastal areas face other direct hazards (e.g. volcanoes, earthquakes, landslides, fires) and also such indirect impacts as reduced production and shipping of resources from the impacted coastal communities. Damage to one society affects us all in this new era of globalization.

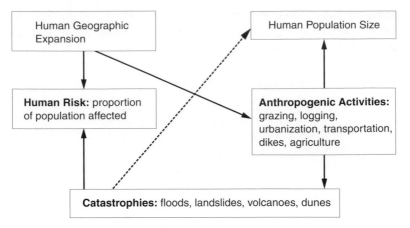

Fig. 1.3  How humans intensify the disastrous effects of natural catastrophes. Solid arrows indicate increasing effects; dashed arrow indicates a retarding effect.

Further, most of the world's active volcanoes are near oceans and can cause underwater landslides that can, and have, resulted in catastrophic tsunamis.

The first, and most tragic, loss from any natural disaster is human life (Table 1.1). More people die, unheralded, from natural disasters than from wars. A second loss is that of property, investments and livelihoods. Obvious direct costs spawned by disturbances such as the Bangladesh floods in 1970, or Hurricane Katrina in the USA in 2005, continue to increase, and the costs even to plan for mitigation of the impacts from these events are staggering. Jobs are lost, people are driven from their homes and lives are devastated. The third type of damage incurred is to the structure, efficiency and productivity of natural ecosystems. Although rarely considered, let alone quantified, these losses are also immense. For example, Hurricane Katrina destroyed over $250\,km^2$ of coastal wetlands, about the size of the Cayman Islands. Multiple natural disasters have a cumulative, destructive impact on natural resources that puts us all at risk. Human activities exacerbate natural disturbances and create novel ones on increasingly large scales. For example, fires and logging destroy several hundred thousand square kilometers of forest per year, an amount of carbon equal to two-thirds of the total carbon emitted by burning fossil fuels. In Europe, $8,000\,km^2$ of forest (an area the size of Cyprus) per year burns, and the size, number and intensity of wildfires is increasing. We face a true crescendo of destruction of our own making.

Table 1.1. *Major natural disturbances in human history. The devastation from volcanoes may be direct or indirect from climatic effects or tsunamis. Earthquakes directly destroy cities, but they may also generate powerful tsunamis, or create huge landslides. Dates are AD except where otherwise noted.*

| Type | Date | Description | Consequences |
|------|------|-------------|--------------|
| Salinization | 1500 BC | Irrigation practices in Indus valley cause crop failures; process is repeated over the millennia | Collapse of earliest civilizations |
| Volcanoes | 1623 BC | Thera (Santorini) explodes; tephra falls | Akrotiri destroyed |
| | 1815 | Tambora (Indonesia), the largest eruption in history | 10,000 killed; ash cloud cools planet leading to further 100,000 deaths from famine and disease |
| | 1902 | Mount Pelée (Martinique) | 30,000 killed by pyroclastic flows |
| Earthquakes | 526 | Antioch (Turkey) | 75,000 killed; weakens Christianity in east |
| | 856 | Corinth (Greece) | 45,000 killed; city abandoned |
| | 1556 | Shanzi Province (China) | 800,000 killed directly; huge toll from landslides |
| | 1755 | Lisbon (Portugal), followed by tsunamis that devastate coastal regions | 100,000 killed; Portuguese influence plummets |
| | 1923 | Kanto Plains (Japan) | 150,000 killed; modern Tokyo reconstructed |
| | 2003 | Bam (Iran) | 23,000 killed in poorly built houses |
| | 2005 | Mountainous Pakistan | 80,000 crushed in building collapses and landslides |
| Tsunamis | 1623 BC | Collapse of Thera caldera causes 150 m tall tsunami | Huge toll; Minoan culture devastated |
| | 1531 | Earthquake triggered; Lisbon (Portugal) | 70,000 killed (30,000 in earthquake) |
| | 1883 | Collapse of Krakatau cone (Indonesia) | 37,000 killed; some climate effects |
| | 2004 | Indian Ocean 9.3 earthquake | 300,000 killed; many communities destroyed |

Table 1.1. (cont.)

| Type | Date | Description | Consequences |
|------|------|-------------|--------------|
| Landslides | 1966 | Mine waste heap collapses at Aberfan (Wales) | 144 people killed |
| | 1998 | Hurricane Mitch (Honduras) | 18,000 people killed (from all impacts) |
| Floods | 1931 | Yellow River (China) | 3.7 million people killed; weakened resistance to invasion by Japan |
| Fires | 64 | Two-thirds of Rome burned | Death toll limited; Christians blamed for destruction |
| | 1666 | London | Most of London burned; a true restoration followed |
| | 1871 | Chicago | 300 killed, but this allowed rejuvenation of city |
| Hurricanes | 1274 | Sea of Japan | 12,000 Mongols killed invading Japan |
| | 1281 | Sea of Japan | 70,000 Mongols killed during second invasion |
| | 1780 | Lesser Antilles (Martinique, Barbados, St. Eustatius) | 20,000 killed |
| | 1900 | Galveston, Texas | 12,000 killed |
| | 1970 | Bangladesh | 500,000 killed by storm surges |
| | 1974 | Honduras (Hurricane Fifi) | 10,000 killed |

Disturbances have altered the course of human history in many ways (Table 1.1). In this book, we will focus on how humans respond to and often intensify the effects of large-scale, natural disturbances such as volcanoes, earthquakes, floods and fires. We will also cover some purely anthropogenic disturbances, such as grazing and mining, that impact landscapes on a large scale. However, we will not discuss natural and human generated disturbances that do little damage to landscapes, even if their impact on humans is enormous (e.g. urban fires, epidemics and famine). We will say little about deliberate destruction, usually associated with warfare. Examples include the massacres that followed the capture of such cities as Milan (by Goths in AD 538),

Jerusalem (by Christians in 1099) and Nanking (by Japanese in 1937–8). The "normal" business of military activity, however, is included. For example, driving heavy vehicles across the landscape destroys vegetation which should be restored.

Disturbances are not all traumatic exclamation points. Many result when the natural ability of an ecosystem to withstand chronic adverse effects and yet remain productive is finally overwhelmed. Many systems will not be able to recover from certain disturbances even when the disturbance ceases. Deforestation and overgrazing are well-known causes of gradual yet severe disturbance. Both processes promote erosion and nutrient losses. Others, less widely appreciated, include accumulating pollutants, siltation of marshes, the gradual desiccation of lakes due to plunging water tables and the filling in of wetlands. We will explore these slowly unfolding disturbances in several places.

We will also describe a few devastating forces from the perspective of how ecosystems respond. In particular, lakes and coastal ecosystems are being subjected to natural disasters, such as hurricanes, and human behaviors that destroy marshes and lakes. As the sole species that is a global geological force, we must accept the duty of stewardship. It has been rare for a society to understand the consequences of chronic disturbances and rarer still for effective policies to be instituted to avert crises. Forces that a healthy society could withstand can destroy a weakened one. To guard against adverse impacts of changing climates and other insidious disturbances such as soil erosion and desertification, ecosystem damage should be avoided and repaired to retain productivity and resilience. Morality aside, it is in our own best interests that we mitigate the effects of both self-imposed and natural disturbances.

Ecology has emerged from the academies to become a discipline that is inextricably tied to the fate of humanity. Concepts such as sustainability and biodiversity are now widely discussed and ecological journals that deal with practical applications are common. Restoration has joined conservation as a scion of ecology. While ecologists know a lot about restoring land, much remains to be learned and translated into action. As is always true, the ability to act has to be combined with the will to act. The will of a society can only be derived from a political and economic calculation that demonstrates that action is more valuable than inaction. We believe that the political will for a broad and comprehensive approach to landscape rehabilitation does not yet exist. While the final reports of endless international conferences are filled with action plans to improve the land, those plans

Fig. 1.4 Cliff dwellings of the Anasazi people at Mesa Verde
(Colorado, USA). These dwellings, now protected in a US National Park
and recognized as a World Heritage Site, housed this native population
for the final 100 years of a rich Pueblo culture that thrived from
AD 600–1300. Abrupt abandonment of the area was likely due to
a combination of drought, crop failure, resource depletion and
overpopulation.

are rarely implemented. We will demonstrate that restoration is a
necessary, though far from sufficient, action to sustain societies,
mitigate foreseeable disturbances and provide opportunities for greater
human well-being. Today, we can make choices. Informed choices
enhance the productivity of ecosystems and promote the stability of a
society. As Jared Diamond convincingly demonstrates in "Collapse," the
wrong choices have led many civilizations to fail. The Babylonians,
Mayans and the Anasazi (Fig. 1.4) were three advanced groups that
disappeared or became ghosts of their former glory due largely to
disturbances after long-term environmental degradation. Many cultures
rose and fell due to low-grade disturbances such as overgrazing or poor
agricultural practices that caused salinization and erosion. Rarely were
signs of gradual decline noted until some extreme event triggered the
crash of the economic basis for the culture in question.

Security can ultimately be defined in ecological terms, and
restoring ecosystems to productivity and health is fundamental to the
security of any society. In these terms, human societies are less secure
now than at any time since the expansion of agriculture. Various threats

exist, not only to particular countries or regions, but also to the globe and to all its inhabitants. The environment, and the magnificent biodiversity that it sustains, is gravely threatened. Direct pressures include conversion of habitats (e.g. forests to farms; farms to deserts), invasions of exotic species, over-harvesting of resources and pollution. Indirect pressures include habitat fragmentation and climate change. We will not survive long on this planet without addressing the urgent issues of ecological security and sustainability.

## 1.2   DISTURBANCE AND RECOVERY

Intense natural disturbances are normal events that can benefit ecosystems. Floods deposit nutrients that in turn support fertile alluvial valleys. Fires rejuvenate soils, help to control diseases and often stimulate new growth. Even volcanoes benefit the landscape by creating fertile land. Indonesia and Sicily, two densely populated regions in the world, were formed by volcanism and their soils retain their fertility even under intensive agriculture. Such disturbances as floods, fires and volcanoes thus initiate cycles of renewal without which the landscape would otherwise degenerate, as nutrients are lost. Very old soils such as are found in Australia and Africa are relatively infertile. The new surfaces that result from disturbance are often more fertile than the surfaces they cover or remove. Under natural conditions, biological colonization and physical weathering repair the devastation spawned by natural disturbances through the process of natural recovery or *ecological succession*.

The key to being able to meet the challenges posed by natural disturbances is an understanding of succession. Ecological succession describes how ecosystems repair themselves after disturbances. Ecologists are developing a deeper understanding of these processes and have learned many of the constraints on natural succession. We can use these lessons to accelerate and improve restoration efforts on devastated land and to improve the economic efficiency of these efforts (Fig. 1.5).

Natural recovery may resurrect an ecosystem if disturbance is within historical bounds. Primary succession is one of the most important ecological processes on the planet (Box 1.1). It results when the biota reclaim newly formed land, often against severe odds. Among the constraints to succession are combinations of infertility, lack of suitable germination sites, lack of soil, drought and the failure of colonists to reach the site. Secondary succession is the recovery from less

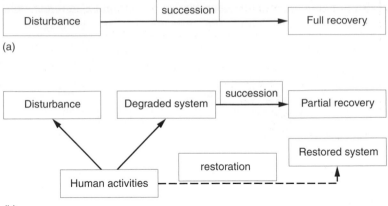

Fig. 1.5 Models of ecosystem dynamics. (a) Natural disturbance followed by ecological succession leads to full recovery. (b) Humans intensify disturbance, permitting only partial recovery, often to a degraded form. Intervention (dashed line) may promote greater recovery and closer approximation of the initial vegetation mosaic.

profound disturbances that allow at least some survivors to reestablish. It is more rapid and less constrained than is primary succession.

Where human impacts are limited, succession can produce intact, fully functional ecosystems, even if they are composed of arrays of species that differ from the pre-disturbance collection. In the contemporary context, where barriers to dispersal and migration abound and where even the air is sometimes toxic, natural recovery is problematic. Normally, renewal includes weathering, nutrient inputs, colonization and habitat improvements both by the colonizing species and others. Today, it is unlikely that unaided recovery can produce natural landscapes. Agriculture *arrests* succession at a young stage so that, when the land is abandoned, it may not recover. Forestry *deflects* succession to more economically productive but biologically impoverished habitats such as tree farms. When forestry ceases, many integral species may not be available in order for succession to proceed unaided.

Humans interact with the disturbance regime of any region by mimicking natural effects (e.g. pavement resembles lava) and altering the frequency (e.g. by fire prevention, flood control) or intensity (e.g. by adjusting grazing levels) of a disturbance. Humans also create unprecedented disturbances of many types (e.g. mine tailings, acid deposition). These alterations make it increasingly unlikely that natural succession can restore damaged landscapes without help.

---

**Box 1.1 How natural systems recover from complete devastation**

Primary succession is the process of ecosystem development on barren surfaces where severe disturbances have removed all life. It requires establishment of a biota adapted to harsh conditions. As physical and biological forces ameliorate conditions, new species arrive, while some pioneers are excluded. Complex systems eventually develop from simple components. The process is influenced by local conditions, context and site history.

All new surfaces are initially devoid of life, so primary succession has been crucial throughout earth's history. Today, all communities of plants, animals and soils are the result of primary succession. It is this process of recovery of ecosystems after disturbance that provides the clean air and water and fertile soils that humans and all organisms need to survive.

When organisms survive the disaster, recovery is called secondary succession. Secondary succession is less dependent on the vagaries of dispersal and is therefore more predictable than primary succession. However, secondary succession in one place can follow several alternative trajectories that depend on chance factors.

Ecologists distinguish autogenic succession, when the mechanisms that drive species change are derived from the organisms within the community (e.g. competition; herbivory) from allogenic succession, when external forces determine species change (e.g. sediment transport from a flood). Change in the early stages of primary succession is due mostly to allogenic mechanisms, but autogenic mechanisms become more important as primary succession proceeds or during secondary succession. Categories such as primary, secondary, autogenic and allogenic denote arbitrary points along environmental gradients and are not easily distinguished.

---

### 1.3   THE FUTURE IS NOW, TIME IS SHORT

Planning and foresight are the keys to long-term survival of modern civilization, yet neither as individuals nor as societies do we plan for the truly worst case. We seem to hope for the best and plan accordingly. We somehow believe that whatever our situation, we are protected from the disasters of the past or accidents in the future. We appear incapable of learning the simple lesson that survival depends on the health of local ecosystems, and that we must nurture these systems. Floods, droughts, volcanoes and earthquakes routinely tip the balance toward chaos. As should by now be clear, there is nothing in our political, social or economic systems that renders our societies immune from the forces of nature. The rules about how resources and disturbances affect civilizations are universal, and a central force in the decline of empires seems to have been a failure to respond effectively to environmental disturbances.

In order to meet the ever-increasing challenges to human welfare posed by the interaction of large-scale natural disturbances with human disturbances and population expansion, we should use every means at our disposal. We no longer have the luxury of letting damaged land recover naturally or to move our projects onto better land. We must maximize productivity of the lands we use and minimize the "down time." While the humans of this planet show an insatiable appetite for resources that often forces ethical considerations to be ignored or rationalized, we believe that wise management of available resources may ease pressures on all resources. One component of wisely managing any system is to foster efficient recovery of devastated ecosystems. Failure to do so will hasten the decline of the quality of life many of us now enjoy and make progress difficult. We can nurse damaged systems to health in many ways. We will sift through a tangle of ecological theory to summarize crucial principles that can aid humanity's greatest challenge – maintaining an acceptable quality of life in the face of escalating environmental degradation. In this book, we focus on ecological tools that are readily available, inexpensive and easily applied to the challenge of promoting recovery from natural disturbances.

BIBLIOGRAPHY

Belnap, J. and Gillette, D. A. (1998). Vulnerability of desert biological soil crusts to wind erosion: the influences of crust development, soil texture, and disturbance. *Journal of Arid Environments*, **39**, 133–42.
Diamond, J. (2005). *Collapse: How Societies Choose to Fail or Succeed*. New York: Penguin Group.
Fagan, B. (1999). *Floods, Famines and Emperors: El Nino and the Fate of Civilizations*. New York: Basic Books.
Fagan, B. (2000). *The Little Ice Age: How Climate Made History*, 1300–1850. New York: Basic Books.
Keys, D. (2000). *Catastrophe: An Investigation into the Origins of the Modern World*. New York: Ballantine Books.

McKibben, B. (1989). *The End of Nature*. New York: Random House.

Oliver-Smith, A. and Hoffman, S.M. eds. (1999). *The Angry Earth*. New York: Routledge.

Pickett, S.T.A. and White, P.S. eds. (1985). *The Ecology of Natural Disturbance and Patch Dynamics*. New York: Academic Press.

Reice, S.R. (2001). *The Silver Lining: The Benefits of Natural Disasters*. Princeton, NJ: Princeton University Press.

# 2

## Natural disturbances: synergistic interactions with humans

Dramatic natural disturbances are sometimes so incomprehensible and so destructive to humans that we blame supernatural beings: lightning is Thor striking his hammer, hurricanes are controlled by Hanaka, volcanoes erupt capriciously at the whim of deities such as Vulcan or Pele, while Poseidon wreaks havoc by flooding dry land. As our understanding of cataclysmic forces such as hurricanes, volcanoes and flooding grows, we begin to grasp some of the mechanics of a disturbance. Progress has been made in predicting weather (especially hurricane trajectories), the likelihood of volcanic eruptions and even the timing and extent of floods. However, there is still much to learn about where, why and when disturbances occur. Some answers lie in global weather patterns or wobbles in the tilt of the earth. Yet, enough mysteries remain that supernatural causes provide attractive explanations for some. Whatever their mechanics, timing or ultimate causes, disturbances are as much a part of our lives as dawn and dusk, as inevitable as winter following autumn. It behooves us to try to understand disturbances in order to mitigate their negative impacts, or at least to learn when it is best to run away and when it is best to stay. Disturbances vary widely in size and destructiveness. They can be as small as one tree falling in your backyard or as large as the 2004 tsunami in the Indian Ocean. In this chapter, we outline the types of disturbance and clarify the definitions of disturbance. We then introduce the disturbed habitats that we discuss in later chapters. Finally, we explore how disturbances interact to create complex short-term and long-term effects on the land.

Fig. 2.1 A vegetated island inundated by flooding in a braided river system, Rakaia River Gorge (Canterbury, New Zealand), December 1989. The yellow-flowered shrub, *Cytisus scoparius*, is an invasive weed common in these habitats. (Courtesy of Rowan P. Buxton).

## 2.2  DISTURBANCE TYPES

Natural disturbances can be described in terms of the four classical elements of wind, earth, water and fire. The powerful winds of hurricanes and tornadoes cause great destruction in tropical and temperate areas respectively (see Plate 2). Even less intense winds can transport sand and bury farms and cities. Dust clouds can affect surrounding regions and even transport diseases and nutrients between continents. Disturbances that involve earth movement (and tectonic activity) include earthquakes, volcanoes (see Plate 3) and landslides. These predominate around the rim of the Pacific Ocean and in central Asia, but earthquakes periodically devastate Europe, Africa and interior North America as well. Landslides occur in mountains and on any steep slope that has become destabilized. Water is a disturbance when glacial ice scours the land or when water is superabundant, as when rivers flood (Fig. 2.1) and sea waves crash across the land. The absence of water is also a disturbance that can occur anywhere, but drought is typical of mid-latitude deserts and steppes. Fire particularly affects coniferous forests (Fig. 2.2), temperate grasslands, temperate shrublands and tropical savannas.

Fig. 2.2  Yellowstone fire (Colorado, USA), five years after the 1988 burns.
Note the habitat variation and regeneration of lodgepole pine.

Many of these disturbances interact. Glaciers melt, destabilize the landscape and cause landslides; landslides dam rivers to create floods; and hurricanes kill trees that then burn. The sum of all disturbances that affect an area is called the disturbance regime. Within one climatic region, there can be a similar disturbance regime, but local variations in smaller scale disturbances are also important.

Overlaying all these natural forces are the overt actions of humans. Agriculture, forestry, mineral extraction, transportation, military activities, urbanization and the encouragement of homogeneous world flora and fauna are major disturbances caused by humanity. When compared with natural disturbances, anthropogenic ones are often more extensive and more severe. For several centuries, humans have been a global geological force, mining mountains and damming rivers. Since the European encounter with the New World, we have also become a global biological force, moving species around the world. Within the last century, we have even become a global meteorological force as our impacts on world climate alter weather patterns, hurricane intensities and even ocean currents. With better technology and more people, the ability to alter the consequences of natural disturbances has increased. Our water pumps sometimes stop lava flows, our bulldozers clear dunes, our roads trigger landslides, our diversions and impoundments of rivers alter floodplains, our matches start forest fires and our domesticated animals graze the earth. We have also created novel disturbances such as the deposition of heavy metals around a smelter. Any discussion of disturbances ought to involve those caused by humans.

## 2.3    DEFINITIONS

We use the term disturbance to mean a relatively discrete event in time and space that alters the structure of populations, communities and ecosystems. Typically, there is a loss of biomass (as when a tree falls down or burns), but sometimes there is just a shift in a physical resource (as when flood waters rise and soil oxygen is depleted). After a disturbance, there is some basic change in the ecosystem (the entire combination of plants, animals and their environment).

As with so much else in ecology, the impact of a disturbance depends on what spatial and temporal scales are considered. A transient disturbance does not usually impact long-term processes or vice versa. For example, a brief and unseasonably late frost that kills a flower will not necessarily kill the entire plant. Likewise, glaciers that return every 100,000 years do not impact a human living within an inter-glacial period. In a similar vein, there are likely to be few interesting consequences of a small disturbance on a large area (one gopher mound on a prairie), nor much need to focus on the impacts of a large disturbance on small-scale processes (a landslide on a seedling). Of course, the importance of an impact is in the eye of the beholder. A raindrop can kill an emerging seedling, a tiny stream can wash away a newly hatched bird and a hurricane can be very important to you if your house is destroyed.

The accumulated impacts of many small, discrete events such as a herbivore eating a leaf or water evaporating from the soil can lead, over time, to major landscape impacts from grazing or salinization. The impacts of such chronic disturbances differ only subtly from ecological stress, where resources are lowered on a regular basis, such as a low tide, a cold winter or a dry summer. In this book, we focus on relatively large-scale disturbances but are aware that local impacts can be significant.

Disturbance is a term that is deliberately general, until carefully defined for a particular purpose. Terms like "disaster" and "catastro-phe" are emotionally laden terms that focus on the negative impacts of a disturbance, generally from a human perspective, but these are not always human-centered. Most would agree that a forest fire is disastrous to a population of deer or that a hurricane can have a catastrophic effect on a coral reef. We will sometimes use the words "disaster" or "catastrophe" when we want to emphasize impacts that are widespread or severe, or when we simply want to focus your attention.

We can further clarify the meaning of "disturbance" by describing its frequency, size and severity. The frequency of a disturbance is measured by its return interval. A patch of forest in Puerto Rico can expect to be hit by a hurricane on average once every 60 years. The size of a disturbance is the extent of its direct and indirect impacts. Lava directly impacts what it physically covers but may extend its indirect influence to nearby trees, heating them until they burst into flame. Some disturbances, such as ash from large volcanoes or human-created pollution, can quickly become airborne and have indirect, global impacts. There is no minimum or maximum limit to the size of a disturbance. Again, it depends on the spatial scale of interest.

Severity is a measure of the degree of impact of a disturbance. How many trees or fish or people were killed is a typical, although sometimes gruesome measure of severity. More subtle usages include how high into the tree canopy fire burns, how much fertility remains in the soil, how long floodwaters remain or how many animals grazed on a pasture. Intensity is a related term that describes the physical force of an event, like the wind speed of a hurricane. Because intensity is usually linked to severity, we use the term severity.

## 2.4   GRADIENTS OF SEVERITY

We organize the remainder of this book around a gradient of decreasing disturbance severity (Table 2.1). We start in Chapter 3 with infertile, unstable habitats, and then proceed to infertile and stable habitats (Chapter 4), fertile, unstable habitats (Chapter 5) and fertile, stable habitats (Chapter 6). We do this for several reasons. First, we want to emphasize the variety of biological legacies left behind by disturbances. Second, we want to show that variety in a coherent fashion. Most importantly, we want to focus on the different responses needed to understand and remediate the consequences of disturbances that vary in severity. Gradients, not categories, characterize natural phenomena. Therefore, our groupings are points on a continuum and are not rigidly defined. Conditions following a given disturbance may vary dramatically depending on local conditions. Influences from the surrounding terrain or the history of disturbance at the site have important effects.

Table 2.1. *Types of natural disturbances discussed. Volcanic ejecta include pyroclastic flows, lahars (mudflows) and air-fall deposits called "tephra."*

|  | Stability | |
|---|---|---|
|  | Low | High |
| Low fertility | **Chapter** 3 | **Chapter** 4 |
|  | Volcanic ejecta | Lava flows |
|  | Dunes | Cliffs |
|  | Glacial forelands |  |
| High fertility | **Chapter** 5 | **Chapter** 6 |
|  | Landslides | Fire |
|  | Floodplains | Hurricanes |
|  | Lakeshores | Grazing |
|  | Marine coastlines |  |

Nevertheless, our categories emphasize key challenges in ecosystem recovery.

The resulting fertility is a good measure of disturbance severity. Both natural recovery and human-aided restoration will be delayed by infertility compared with recovery on a fertile site. We imply various conditions when we use the terms infertile and fertile. A disturbance that leaves little or no soil produces infertile conditions. Fertile sites will have adequate nutrients, water and sunlight. We indirectly imply other factors that favor growth, such as abundant pollinators for plants, or food, shelter, nest sites and mates for animals. Our perspective is, however, focused on the landscape level and not on individuals. Therefore, a fertile (favorable) habitat might be locally unfavorable for some organisms. For example, some fire-adapted plants sprout vigorously after fire and capitalize on high nutrient availability in the ashes. For them, the site is very fertile. Meanwhile, other plants may be delayed until nutrients are incorporated into a new organic soil and do not experience the site as fertile.

Stability is not as closely tied to severity as is fertility but stability still appears to impact most recovery processes. Unstable sites can be caused by continual disturbance, as when a landslide re-slides or a dune advances across the landscape. If this instability is severe enough, root establishment, animal nesting, nutrient accumulation and many other variables will be thwarted. Some organisms can colonize unstable surfaces, but extensive ecosystem development is usually delayed until the surfaces become stable.

## 2.5   INFERTILE HABITATS

In Chapter 3, we address recovery processes on infertile, unstable habitats produced by severe disturbances. We consider these conditions to be the most difficult for natural succession and succession aided by restoration efforts. Volcanic deposits other than lava are the first type of disturbance we address. These include three categories of materials. Both pyroclastic flows (hot gas–solid mixtures) and lahars (cool, more or less fluid mixtures) flow down the volcanic slopes. Tephra is fine-textured ash, scoria or pumice that is blown into the air, later falling to earth. Dunes, our second type of disturbance, are also infertile and unstable, with generally slow development of organic matter. Finally, when glaciers melt (as most are now doing), they leave behind a relatively infertile and certainly unstable terrain of scoured rock and unconsolidated silt. Rain, river water, glacial rebound and landslides start the process of stabilizing such post-glacial terrain. Recovery on all these infertile, unstable habitats is slow, especially in cold, dry sites. Exceptions do occur, as when volcanic deposits are thin or dunes and glacial moraines are stable. If the disturbed area is small, narrow or surrounded by dense, easily dispersed species, recovery will be more rapid.

Chapter 4 considers habitats left infertile but stable. Lava flows are a classic example, providing the most sterile substrates in Nature. However, as we discuss, they are not sterile for long and colonization can be more rapid than on other forms of volcanic surfaces, especially when organic matter accumulates in cracks in the lava. Cliffs result from tectonic movement along plates, river erosion or sometimes from human activities such as quarrying for rocks and excavating mines. Cliffs are relatively stable but highly infertile surfaces where colonization is limited to a few microsites where soil and moisture can accumulate. Nonetheless, cliffs support a marvelous diversity of plants and animals.

## 2.6   FERTILE HABITATS

Fertile habitats provide better conditions for growth and recovery. First, we address fertile habitats that remain unstable (Chapter 5). These unstable habitats include landslides, floodplains, lakeshores and ocean margins. Under these conditions, plant colonists often grow quickly but die from renewed disturbances, thus resetting the successional processes of recovery. This instability also can reduce local fertility, leading to heterogeneous resource availability as found on landslides or river floodplains.

Landslides vary widely in the degree of soil remaining and therefore in their fertility after a disturbance. Much depends on the initial fertility and depth of the soils that slid as well as on the stability of the final slope. Infertile, high-elevation gravels that keep re-sliding from new contributions higher on a mountain will be slower to revegetate than fertile forest soils that fall only a short distance and leave an organic-rich mix deposited at the base of the slide. River floodplains also present an intermediate case. Some river water is rich in nutrients from upstream sources and its silts retain these nutrients when they spread out over a wide floodplain. Other narrow rivers deposit coarse, infertile gravels where recovery will be much slower and renewed disturbance more likely. Lakeshores and ocean shorelines provide other examples of variable habitats that are relatively fertile but unstable. Each is subject to damage from external forces. Lakes can dry out if their sources are reduced or eliminated, leading to dusty or salty expanses. Ocean shores, particularly in estuaries, are subject to rapid sedimentation from changes in the hydrology of the supporting rivers, and to erosion.

Chapter 6 covers disturbances that provide the most favorable conditions for recovery because the sites are relatively fertile and stable. Although there are many examples of such disturbances, we focus on fire, hurricanes, strong winds and the impacts of severe grazing. Fires can be devastating when they burn through all organic matter and lead to severe soil erosion. However, most fires leave the soil and even many plant parts undamaged. Remaining roots can keep the burned habitat from eroding. Similarly, strong winds such as hurricanes and tornadoes do not usually disrupt roots enough to cause extensive soil erosion. Exceptions occur, of course, and the accompanying rains (rather than the winds) can cause extensive landslides as in Central America following Hurricane Mitch in 1998. Finally, grazing adds fertility to some soils, but it disrupts plant growth. Severe grazing over extended periods causes erosion, but the immediate impact is simply soil compaction and removal of aboveground biomass. Fertility and stability remain at relatively high levels in these three types of disturbance and recovery processes are faster than for the other disturbances we discuss.

We focus on large-scale, natural disturbances that impact land-scape level processes, but do not ignore other types of disturbance. Earthquakes did not merit a special section because their impacts and severity are hard to categorize. Instead, we discuss earthquakes indirectly through the secondary disturbances that they often trigger, particularly landslides. Although we discuss large-scale grazing impacts, animals also have many local impacts such as excavating burrows, but these impacts are usually at a smaller scale than is our focus. Finally, human analogies to natural disturbances are discussed throughout the book. These are fascinating and important, given the increasing human influence on the planet.

## 2.7   DISTURBANCE INTERACTIONS AND LINKAGES WITH HUMANS

The cycle of interactions between natural disasters and human pressures guarantees future catastrophes. Global warming, one manifestation of increasing human effects on the biosphere, is apparently having many effects on the frequency and intensity of natural disasters. Fire severity has been predicted to increase for much of the USA because warmer conditions combined with drought are a likely result of global warming over much of the planet. Drought itself is predicted to expand and intensify for several reasons. Higher temperatures lead to an earlier start of the growing season, which leads to greater loss of water from plants and soils (evapotranspiration), thus creating later season drought stress in many systems. Storms of all types are predicted to increase their severity. Hurricanes (see below), tornadoes, windstorms and ice storms are all expected to become more frequent and stronger as global warming continues. Even landslides are expected to become more common. More rapid melting of snow and glacial retreat create landslides. Landslides occur more frequently if humans have destabilized slopes through road building or logging. In addition to being triggered by earthquakes and volcanoes, landslides are frequently triggered by soil saturation so regions expected to receive greater precipitation are likely to experience a greater frequency of landslides. In addition to these disturbance effects, global warming is likely to stimulate the expansion of undesirable exotic species and diseases.

In Fig. 2.3, we highlight a few ways in which natural disturbances interact with the activities of humans. Global warming is real and almost certainly has a strong anthropogenic component. The diagram shows only a few links among types of natural disasters that impact agriculture, though there are many cascading effects. For example, as global temperatures increase, patterns of monsoons are altered, creating more intense droughts and, in combination with overgrazing,

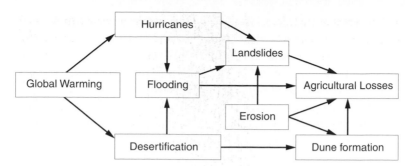

Fig. 2.3 An example of how natural disturbances are intertwined and intensified by human actions. Arrows indicate an increase in the severity or frequency of the targeted box. Many other interactions occur.

desertification. Drought weakens plants, exposing them to pathogens and reducing their vigor. Dry vegetation with a large proportion of dead plants will promote intense fires that expose the landscape to erosion and slides. Increasingly arid lands are prone to wind erosion, leading to an intensification of dune formation. Together, these events cause increasing losses to agriculture, as well as to basic infrastructure. Finally, increasing hurricane intensity directly impacts tropical crops and indirectly destroys agricultural land through landslides in mountainous regions. Four detailed examples follow that illustrate the complexity of disturbance interactions and the interplay between humans and disturbance.

The massive earthquake in the Indian Ocean on December 26, 2004 triggered a devastating tsunami, painfully demonstrating how disturbances can be linked. Despite the enormity of the earthquake (Richter scale 9.3), earthquake damage was minor compared to that done by the resulting tsunami. These horrendous sea waves, easily the worst since 1908 (Messina and Reggio di Calabria, Italy), caused around 300,000 human deaths and untold devastation. Linked disasters of this magnitude would be devastating under any circumstance, but as is so often true, human actions exacerbated the calamity in several ways. Coral reefs had been dynamited in many parts of Indonesia and Sri Lanka to improve shipping, and mangroves had been converted to shrimp nurseries, housing and tourist activities. In the areas where coral reefs and mangroves had been removed, tsunami damage was greater than in areas where they were still intact because less of the storm's energy was absorbed. Salty water flowed many kilometers inland and ruined many coastal crops. In the aftermath, surviving forests were decimated to provide materials to replace lost homes and boats, while exotic species that were washed inland are now establishing with unknown consequences for native plants and animals.

Humans sometimes sow the seeds for dramatic catastrophes spawned by natural events. The Vaiont Dam in the Veneto region of Italy remains one of the highest in the world. Finished in 1961, it functioned only briefly before torrential rains triggered a huge landslide into the reservoir. Deforestation of the hills above the dam caused this landslide, which, like a boulder tossed into a swimming pool, caused a wave 250 m tall that easily breached the dam. The flood destroyed at least five villages and killed over 3,000 people. While the dam still stands, the reservoir contains only the rubble from this huge landslide.

In some cases, humans simply ignore scientific warnings, and rush heedlessly into calamity. The Teton Dam in Idaho was rushed to completion by the political clout of local agricultural interests and the cooperative US Bureau of Reclamation, over the strong warnings by the US Geological Survey that the site was unstable. The dam began to fill in late 1975. On June 5, 1976, immediately after the reservoir had filled, the nearly 100 m tall dam failed, unleashing a wall of water such as had not been seen since the ice dam of glacial Lake Missoula failed about 12,000 years ago. Eleven people died and many towns suffered damage. However, because the failure was gradual, damage was mitigated. The flood was entirely the result of a rush to complete a project without attending to potential problems.

In 1991, tephra deposits from the eruption of Mt. Pinatubo in the Philippines produced widespread havoc. The large floods, pyroclastic deposits and mudflows (Fig. 2.4) spawned by this eruption killed over 25,000 people and had huge economic consequences including the destruction of many villages, reforestation projects and rice farms. These effects persist. Hardest hit were about 10,000 members of the Aeta group living on the volcano. The ancestors of this indigenous people had fled the Spanish in the sixteenth century and resettled on the slopes of Mt. Pinatubo to salvage their way of life. Thus, centuries-old social factors placed these people in harm's way. They were evacuated before the eruption and most have not been able to return. By ill fortune, a typhoon struck the Philippines at the same time, resulting in a bizarre interaction with the volcano. Though excellent early warnings of the impending eruption saved many lives, the death toll rose because, as the rain-soaked ash descended, many roofs collapsed under its weight. This resulted in more deaths than did direct volcanic effects.

Recently, the hurricane season has lengthened and hurricanes have become more intense, due to widespread warming of tropical

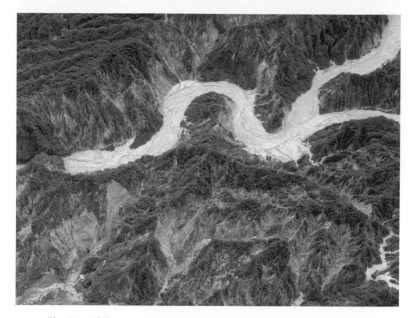

Fig. 2.4 A lahar spawned by Mt. Pinatubo pyroclastic materials on the Sacobia River (Philippines) in 1993. (Courtesy of Thomas Marler.)

oceans. As humans expand into sensitive coastal habitats, natural protective barriers including swamps, dunes and estuaries are being destroyed. Homes continue to be built on marginal land such as coastal bluffs and cliffs or on steep hillsides, resulting in more damage to property and greater loss of human lives. Most dramatically, sea levels are rising, leading to widespread flooding and potential loss of entire nations. Melting glaciers and rising sea levels alter the distribution of the mass of all that water across the land and these shifts can trigger volcanic activity and underwater landslides. Both the natural and human-mediated damage to the land must be mitigated whenever and wherever possible. However, natural recovery is increasingly at the mercy of biogeographic factors that determine the availability of species to invade devastated landscapes. The biota of the planet has been on the move with increasing rapidity since 1492 when Europeans reached America, altering the pathways of natural recovery. The intensity and nature of disturbances have also changed, so that natural recovery is becoming less and less possible. As ecosystems are subjected to multiple stresses, their interacting effects can lead to new kinds of systems incapable of returning to their original state. Increasing fire frequency, habitat fragmentation, greater drought and the invasion of exotic species can combine to form biologically impoverished, degraded ecosystems incapable of recovery. Humans are obligated to fill the breach and guide ecosystem recovery after disturbances.

BIBLIOGRAPHY

Daily, G.C. ed. (1997). *Nature's Services: Societal Dependence on Natural Ecosystems.* Washington, DC: Island Press.
Friday, L. and Lasky, R. (1989). *The Fragile Environment.* Cambridge: Cambridge University Press.
McGuire, B. (2006). Earth, fire and fury. *New Scientist,* **190,** 32–6.
Walker, L.R. ed. (1999). *Ecosystems of Disturbed Ground. Ecosystems of the World, No. 16.* Amsterdam: Elsevier.
Walker, L.R. and del Moral, R. (2003). *Primary Succession and Ecosystem Rehabilitation.* Cambridge: Cambridge University Press.

Plate 1 Overgrazing by goats in the Mediterranean (here in Sicily) over millennia has reduced woodlands to scrublands. Continued grazing and land degradation preclude natural recovery.

Plate 2 Devastated forest in Puerto Rico. Periodic violent winds wreak widespread damage on vegetation. (Courtesy of Ariel E. Lugo.)

Plate 3  Hawaiian pahoehoe. Lava slowly spreads into a forest on Kilauea volcano, burning what it does not smother.

Plate 4  Lupines on Mount St. Helens. Despite their limited dispersal ability, lupines were often the first colonizers, where they facilitated the establishment of other species. Here, mosses were the primary beneficiaries, but they form a dense mat that inhibits the colonization of seed plants.

Plate 5 Fox Glacier (South Island, New Zealand). The nitrogen-fixing shrub New Zealand broom (*Carmichaelia*) colonizes the young gravel moraine in front of this steep, coastal glacier.

Plate 6 The view from Vulcan's forge. The island of Vulcano, off the coast of Sicily, provides an escape from the hectic pace of large Italian cities. Here we find long history, limited tourism and agriculture and, according to some, the path to perdition.

Plate 7 The Three Sisters, Blue Mountains (New South Wales, Australia). These cliffs represent three beautiful sisters of the Katoomba tribe who fell in love with three brothers of a forbidden tribe. They were turned into these cliffs for their own protection, by a shaman who, unfortunately, was killed before he could reverse the spell.

Plate 8 Puffin colonies on Latrabjarg Cliff (Breidafjordur, western Iceland). Among the many seabirds that find refuge on cliffs, these birds are unusual because they are adept underwater swimmers.

Plate 9 Cliffs along the Great Ocean Road (Victoria, Australia). These magnificent sedimentary cliffs were formed by active wind and water erosion. Coastal cliffs provide sand for beaches many kilometers distant.

Plate 10 Athel (*Tamarix aphylla*) and other tamarisk species commonly invade such barren lakeshores where water levels fluctuate greatly. These "salt cedars" use water lavishly, intensify desertification by lowering the water table and often deposit salt on the soil surface. (Courtesy of Willard E. Hayes, II).

Plate 11 Montane lakes demonstrate typical zonation patterns (Washington State, USA). Submerged, floating and emergent herbs dominate the shallow water, while wetland shrubs occur where soil is saturated, but rarely flooded. These patterns inform wetland restoration.

Plate 12 Mangroves in the Florida Keys (USA). The roots (called pneumatophores) provide oxygen to parts of the plants buried in the silt, while the dense tangle of roots anchors the swamp and protects the inland areas.

Plate 13 Forest fire in Kakadu National Park (Northern Territory, Australia). Intentional fires have long been set by native Aboriginals in Australia during the end of the wet season to avoid hotter, more destructive fires during the dry season. These fires also promote palatable grasses and thereby improve hunting for wallabies and other grazers attracted by the grass.

Plate 14 Hurricane Hugo (1989) severely damaged rainforests (Puerto Rico). Immediately following the hurricane the forest was a jumble of defoliated stems and toppled trees, yet small palms and many epiphytes survived. The forest regeneration was rapid because, though damaged, most trees survived.

Plate 15 The restoration of the Lehigh Gap zinc smelter impacts (Pennsylvania, USA). Eighty years of sulfur and heavy metals had created a desert in this eastern Pennsylvania region. For 20 years, the site was an unproductive eyesore. Starting in 2001, restoration that used naturalistic methods has produced a young, but functional community dominated by a diversity of grasses. (Courtesy of Dan Kunkle).

Plate 16 Crissey Field dunes (San Francisco, California, USA). These artificial dunes were constructed to protect a restored salt marsh and to withstand intense human use. Native species were used exclusively and the dune vegetation resembles that found in undisturbed areas north of the site. The site was two years old when the image was taken.

# 3

# Infertile and unstable habitats

Some of the most dramatic landscapes on earth scarcely support life because they are infertile and unstable. Infertility limits growth and instability limits establishment. These neglected, barren habitats of our world once escaped human impact because of their isolation and because productive habitats were more profitable. Today, humans are creating similarly impoverished habitats, but unlike natural ones, human-created barrens are close to human habitats and less productive. Due to the continuing global loss of usable habitat, these unproductive environments could be restored for human use.

Volcanoes, moving sands and glaciers all form infertile and unstable habitats. In the aftermath of violent cataclysms, volcanoes can create unstable surfaces such as lahars and scoria. The slow advance of sterile sand dunes across the landscape has both beneficial and catastrophic aspects. While coastal dunes protect the shores, interior dunes are expanding at alarming rates to threaten many communities and ruin pastoral lands. However, many interior dunes also support rare and complex ecosystems. The grinding, global retreat of glacial ice reveals jumbled barrens. The biota colonizes these inhospitable sites only with difficulty and persistence. Plants and animals eventually colonize the empty habitats formed by volcanoes, dunes and melting glaciers and when they do their success offers lessons for restoration of similar infertile and unstable habitats. In this chapter, we explore the constraints to establishment on these severely altered ecosystems and suggest that even they have value for sustaining economies and easing pressure on other habitats.

## 3.2  POROUS VOLCANIC MATERIALS

### 3.2.1  Introduction

Volcanoes created much of the land found on the planet today. In fact, volcanoes are still forming new land. On the Island of Hawaii, Kilauea Volcano has erupted continuously since 1983 and has buried over $102 \, km^2$, including roads and villages, while adding over $2 \, km^2$ to the island. Volcanoes produce enormous sporadic eruptions, often with catastrophic results. Humanity has confronted these unpredictable and terrible forces by creating many explanatory stories. Today, humans are forced to interact with these captivating volcanic forces in many ways because an increasing share (12 percent) of the world's population lives on or near a volcano that has erupted within the last 10,000 years. Of these 1,410 volcanoes, 457 have at least one million people living within 100 km, while only 300 are in relatively uninhabited regions. Population densities around volcanoes that have erupted in historical times are about six times that of population densities in all inhabited land, so the problem is far from trivial. Populations tend to be higher on the fertile slopes of tropical volcanoes such as those in the Philippines and Indonesia, and lower in temperate locations such as Chile and Japan.

When the Osceola mudflow occurred on Mt. Rainier (Washington, USA) about 5,600 years ago, the destruction of $800 \, km^2$ of forests and river valleys probably did not kill a single human. Today, a similar event is thought likely to occur, but over 500,000 people and billions of dollars worth of developed land are at risk. Most young volcanoes slumber unobtrusively on the edges of our consciousness, yet we retain a deep, primal awe of their potential fury. Then they erupt.

Although lava is the best-known product of volcanoes, it forms stable surfaces. Here we address less familiar but equally important volcanic products that produce surfaces that often drain rapidly and are infertile. They are subject to erosion that frequently eliminates plants struggling to establish, thus "resetting" the succession clock. Despite these limitations, ecological recovery can be more rapid than on lava because seedlings often do establish and nutrients can be introduced from adjacent habitats. How does this occur?

### 3.2.2  Physical setting

Three types of porous volcanic surfaces may be created during a single eruption. They can act or local, regional and even global scales. The most intense are pyroclastic flows or *nuée ardentes* (Box 3.1). These searing

Box 3.1  **This young land**

Pyroclastic avalanches devastate all life. In 1980, Roger landed on a flow deposited two months before and found the deep, dusty powder whipping about and into his throat as he sank up to his knees in 50°C powder. After 25 years, though far from fully recovered, this pyroclastic flow supports a rich flora and fauna, ripe for the establishment of forest tree species. How did this transformation occur?

Fig. 3.1  Pyroclastic plains on Mount St. Helens (Washington, USA), June 1980. The dusty powder buried the landscape to depths over 30 m. However, within a year, wind and water had removed most of this material, allowing succession to commence.

blasts of incandescent mixtures of volcanic materials and superheated gas sweep down volcanic slopes to destroy all in their path. They are the swiftest and most devastating type of volcanic event, first noted in AD 79 by Pliny the Younger, who watched the elder Pliny become the most famous victim of Mt. Vesuvius near Pompeii. Pyroclastic flows leave behind dusty plains covered with a powder that resembles fly ash (Fig. 3.1). Natural recolonization is slow and requires stabilization and the development of fertility. Their true nature was not appreciated until 1902 when Mt. Pelée on Martinique produced deadly pyroclastic flows that killed 30,000 inhabitants of St. Pierre. The sole survivor, a prisoner locked in a dungeon, was driven mad. He gained notoriety by being displayed in P. T. Barnum's circus.

A second type of nonporous volcanic deposit is derived from colder, massive, wet avalanches. These rivers of mud, called by their Indonesian name lahar, form in several ways. Normally, they result from the extremely rapid melting of glaciers and snow during an eruption. The mass of water picks up everything in its path to form a slurry that sweeps down river valleys, often scouring the valley and expanding onto the floodplain. Lahars also develop from *debris avalanches*, which occur when the flank of a steep mountain, usually a volcano, collapses and plummets downslope. As the heavy boulders, rocks and trees are deposited and the proportion of water in the mass increases, lahars form. These devastating walls of rock, debris and water clog valleys and destroy forests, bridges, villages and all else in their paths. In rare cases, melting snow forms a perched lake dammed by rubble. When the dam breaks, a sudden and unexpected lahar occurs. Large debris avalanches may travel many kilometers before coming to rest, or they may transform into lahars, which can travel many tens of kilometers downstream. Because many volcanoes are steep-sided, the force of gravity impels huge volumes down existing river valleys or as a "blanket flow" across the landscape. Lahars are more common at high latitudes and at high elevations, such as in the Andes or equatorial Africa, where heavy snow packs abound. Lahars include reworked rocks and soil, so they are more fertile than other volcanic surfaces. Because they are usually narrow and surrounded by vegetation, they are more easily reached by dispersing organisms.

The final type of porous material created by volcanoes is called tephra. Fire blasting from the throat of volcanoes in explosive Plinean eruptions can carry the tephra several kilometers into the atmosphere, so tephra deposits are the most widespread of volcanic phenomena. Tephra can fall as *lapilli* (small, rounded to angular stone fragments measuring 2−64 mm in diameter) near the volcano or as fine ash that can fall hundreds of kilometers away. Where they land is determined by the prevailing winds during the eruption. During the 1907 eruption of Mt. Ksudach in Kamchatka, only strong southerly winds blew, producing narrow, deep plumes of tephra that extended for over 200 km. Twenty kilometers north of the crater, the deposits were over 5 m thick, easily obliterating the birch forest (Fig. 3.2). However, this depth attenuated rapidly at right angles to the wind, so that some plants survived within 3 km of the center of the deposit (Fig. 3.3).

Fig. 3.2  Tephra from Mt. Ksudach (Kamchatka, Russia). As you move away from the axis of tephra deposition, the vegetation cover on the tephra increases dramatically. This resulted because the roots of woody plants could reach soil if the deposit was less than about 30 cm.

Fig. 3.3  Shallow tephra from Mt. Ksudach (Kamchatka, Russia). Trees are dominated by birches, with snags of trees that died slowly after the 1907 eruption.

> **Box 3.2  Pliny died at Pompeii**
>
> The first well-documented volcanic eruption was that of Vesuvius in
> AD 79, which formed the time capsules at Pompeii and
> Herculaneum. The great Roman admiral and naturalist, Pliny the
> Elder (Gaius Plinius Secundus), died while simultaneously trying to
> save refugees and describe the event. His nephew, Pliny the
> Younger, a callow youth at the time, described the events accurately
> 25 years later. He too nearly perished in tephra falls, but survived
> and saved his mother. Several earthquakes and a small tsunami
> heralded the eruption, which triggered the first described "Plinean
> plume" complete with huge static electrical discharges, followed by
> falls of hot cinders and stones and pyroclastic flows that reached the
> sea. Pliny the Elder was overwhelmed by sulfurous fumes near
> the shore while still trying to observe the eruption of Vesuvius.
> His bravery and determined curiosity come through clearly in
> his nephew's accounts.

Plants and animals will invade each of these types of surfaces after
physical processes such as erosion create microsites for germination
and increase heterogeneity. Sometimes buried organisms survive and,
if exposed, will recolonize a site. Creeks and rivers soon purge their
banks of pyroclastic, lahar and tephra deposits, so that effects on narrow
valleys are short-term. However, across broad landscapes, recolonization
may be slow and sporadic.

### 3.2.3   Volcanoes in the lives of humans

Volcanoes provide windows into the past. Earthquakes, tephra, pyroclastic flows and the associated tsunamis that devastated Crete
produced the earliest record of volcanoes changing history, although
Vesuvius (AD 79; Box 3.2) is certainly the best known ancient eruption.
Volcanoes have destroyed entire civilizations, not just scattered unfor-
tunate populations. Archeological studies of the eruption of Thera in
about 1623 BC showed how it devastated the Minoan culture, probably
stimulated the Atlantis myth and may be the source of the three days
of darkness during which the enslaved Jews escaped Egypt (described
in the book of Exodus of the Old Testament). During the seventeenth
century, at least four episodes of extreme cooling occurred due to
huge eruptions of the little known Huaynaputina (Peru) that rivaled

that of Krakatau. Huaynaputina's distinctive ash has been found in Antarctic and Greenland ice cores. Periodic eruptions during the Little Ice Age (*c.* 1300 to 1850) made an already cooler earth even more inhospitable. Laki (Iceland) created a huge fissure eruption in 1783 that dealt a severe blow to European economies, nearly eliminated Iceland's agriculture and caused the deaths of 20 percent of the Icelandic population. The massive eruption of Tambora on Sumbawa, Indonesia in 1815 was the largest in recorded history. It led to a year without summer, killed at least 100,000 people and obliterated the entire population of humans speaking Tamboran, a language discovered by Europeans only five years before it became extinct. Krakatau, an island in the Sunda Strait of Indonesia, erupted in 1883 with one of the five most devastating eruptions in history, rivaling Tambora. The eruption and associated tsunamis killed over 30,000 people. Within hours of the eruption, witnesses communicated their findings around the world by the recently installed oceanic cables, marking the start of the global information network.

In 1902, Soufrière, on St. Vincent, produced devastating pyroclastic flows and killed about 2,000 people. Nearby, in the same year, Mt. Pelée spawned pyroclastic flows that killed 30,000 people who took refuge in St. Pierre on Martinique. Many volcanoes have erupted under the unsuspecting feet of local people either ignorant of the concept "volcano" or unaware that the giant was sleeping, not dead. Then there are long-distance, stealth volcanoes. For example, lahars spawned by the Andean volcano Nevado del Ruiz (Colombia) in 1985 devastated villages over 100 km from the volcano. Though the eruption itself was small, it killed over 25,000 people, most of whom had no idea that there had been an eruption. Steep topography accelerated the lahars and erosion enhanced their size, thus minimizing any warning and intensifying the havoc. The prehistoric Osceola lahar presumably startled many people because it struck at a great distance with no warning.

The consequences of ash in the upper atmosphere include global cooling and disruption of agriculture. Unknown to Europeans, Mt. Taupo in New Zealand (AD 186) and Krakatau in Indonesia (*c.* AD 535) significantly cooled the atmosphere and reduced agricultural yields. The historical perspectives about climate fluctuations now being gained from studies of ice cores suggest that changes of broad amplitude have been the norm and that civilizations would be wise to plan for such changes in the future. Several twentieth century events, such as Mt. Katmai (Alaska, 1912) and Mt. Pinatubo (Philippines, 1991) have caused spikes of global cooling. Volcanoes also produce fertile land.

From Indonesia to Italy, from Chile to Alaska, from Kamchatka to New Zealand and from Rwanda to Tanzania, dense populations are supported by unusually fertile volcanic soils. Mt. Etna, a dangerous and looming presence, is central to the economy of eastern Sicily. Abundant citrus orchards and quality vineyards clothe the lower slopes, nourished by nearly constant ash falls. Although Sicilians respect Etna, summer homes continue to encroach on the slopes despite constant tephra deposits, to say nothing of the threat of major lava flows.

Volcanoes support ecotourism in such diverse sites as Mt. Kilimanjaro in east Africa, Mt. Ruapehu in New Zealand, Mt. Tolbachik in Kamchatka, Mt. Hekla in Iceland and the many active volcanoes in Japan, Alaska and the northwestern USA. Climbers love the challenges of volcanoes (e.g. Mt. Rainier, Washington); others ascend volcanoes for religious reasons (e.g. Mt. Fuji, Japan). Skiers seek adventure on volcanoes in many parts of the world. Particularly when volcanoes are in eruptive phases, they attract tourists seeking excitement.

The devastating impacts described above have another positive aspect. They provide many ecological lessons that we can apply to efficient restoration of surfaces created by human actions. Natural recovery from a volcanic disaster involves stabilization, dispersal, establishment and facilitation. These processes are the foundation of rehabilitation of anthropogenic sites. In 1916, the science of plant ecology received a major stimulus when the American R. F. Griggs reached what he called the "Valley of 10,000 Smokes". Though it had been four years since the eruption of Mount Katmai, one of the largest in history, Griggs was met with a barren landscape. Tephra reached Vancouver, Canada and pyroclastic flows filled valleys to depths of more than 100 m. The crater of Katmai collapsed to form a caldera, now a lake. Over the years, Griggs reported many unique observations that helped advance our understanding of succession.

### 3.2.4  Ecological responses

The study of natural recovery on soft volcanic surfaces has intrigued many ecologists, including both of us, and we have studied responses of the biota on several volcanoes. In general, our studies and those of colleagues have led to several conclusions.

Succession on soft volcanic surfaces is relatively unpredictable and is subject to several chance factors. It is dependent on local factors that control plant growth rates and the proximity to sources of colonists. Initially powdery and unstable, pyroclastic deposits are molded by physical processes. Rain helps to compact them and wind removes fine particles, leaving behind pumice rocks that stabilize the surface, mulch the surface and create safe-sites for germination. Wind also creates favorable microsites and introduces organic matter from dust, spores and insects that increases fertility. These marginally more favorable microsites become centers for plant establishment and slow growth. As water reworks the site to create rills, more opportunities for seeds appear. Along the rill edges, seeds are protected from wind and have better moisture conditions. Because dispersal favors small, buoyant seeds that cannot survive in harsh conditions, these physical forms of site improvement are critical to starting succession. If nitrogen-fixing species become established, and as wind and animals import more nutrients, succession accelerates.

Colonization requires dispersal, a process that is strongly conditioned by chance and by the location of potential invaders. Early colonists are normally wind-dispersed, and can include mosses and ferns, but success rates differ strongly between the colonists. There is some predictability in the types of species that invade soft volcanic substrates. We have noted a shift in dominance from readily dispersed, short-lived species to those that reach the site and spread effectively by vegetative means. In time, perennials that spread at ground level are replaced by taller shrubs and eventually by trees (if the climate permits trees). Refugia, local sites where some plants have survived, have only minimal impact on the surroundings. Often the species that have survived in a particularly protected site are incapable of expanding into the new environment. However, able colonists reach these fertile oases, establish and deposit copious seeds into the immediate surroundings.

Establishment depends on the formation of safe-sites where seedlings might survive. However, safe-sites also degenerate over time due to weathering and the presence of larger plants. We have noted that the order of establishment can affect subsequent community development. Terrestrial plant ecologists have only recently observed such priority effects, which are frequently reported in marine systems.

Once species are established, they expand, and there is a positive feedback mechanism. The pace of development accelerates over time, but slows with elevation. Sites that were once barren and repeatedly disturbed can begin to develop when the surface becomes stable. Then, because seed sources are very close, development is faster.

Nitrogen-fixing species such as alders, the New Zealand shrub tutu (*Coriaria*) and lupines generally improve soil, but they have complex

Fig. 3.4 Lupines dominate vegetation on Mount St. Helens. This site on a ridge near the crater of Mount St. Helens demonstrates development when lupines invade quickly. Within 15 years, cover of vegetation was nearly 100 percent, whereas plots only 100 m higher in elevation developed much more slowly and remained essentially barren by 2006.

interactions with other species. While soil fertility may be improved, the competitive effects of these species may filter the species that could benefit. Lupines on Mount St. Helens initially formed sporadic, dense colonies that lacked other plants (Fig. 3.4). Because this species is short-lived and susceptible to attack from insects in several ways, the colonies expanded slowly and experienced large cycles of abundance. After a few cycles, species able to establish during "down" years have become abundant. Some of these, especially mosses, make it difficult for large-seeded species to establish (Plate 4).

The rate of succession is governed by how fast biomass can accumulate in the face of abiotic and biotic constraints. Drought, extreme temperatures and the length of the growing season all affect succession in one area. Succession does not often develop toward a single type of vegetation; instead, development paths (trajectories) are varied and can lead to alternative, stable vegetation types. Recent succession on volcanoes has led to different results from earlier succession. This is due to human alterations of the landscape, making a return to the original vegetation unlikely. Habitats are now fragmented (thus creating dispersal barriers) and many regions are dominated by exotic species. Deterministic factors such as competitive dominance could produce predictable results, but they develop slowly.

### 3.2.5 Human responses

Natural recovery of infertile, unstable volcanic substrates is usually left to natural succession. However, there are some cases where recovery of volcanic habitats can be hastened by attention to the lessons learned from Nature. Such applied succession or restoration is increasingly crucial as humans expand into volcanic habitats. In the Philippines, restoration efforts on lahars spawned by the eruption of Mt. Pinatubo (1991) and subsequent torrential rains used insights gained from the study of lahars on Mount St. Helens to hasten the return of rice agriculture in an economically depressed region.

In 1980, the United States Department of Agriculture (USDA) Soil Conservation Service seeded mixtures of exotic species, legumes and fertilizer over much of Mount St. Helens in a misguided effort to control erosion. This effort cost over US$2 million, yet erosion was not reduced and conifer regeneration was impeded. Today, widespread, aerial broadcasting of seeds has been replaced by subtler methods using native species. For example, Professor Akira Miyawaki has led many reforestation projects in Japan and Southeast Asia that provide a benchmark for other projects (Fig. 3.5). He contacts local "green groups," government organizations and the relevant corporations to get sufficient numbers of volunteers. Having determined from his considerable expertise the appropriate species and planting design, he arranges for the proper number and species of trees to be delivered to the site on the appointed day. Materials are usually donated, but may also be purchased with contributions from a variety of sources.

There are many habitats created by humans that are analogous to volcanic sites and which can be restored using ecological principles. Some, such as abandoned gravel roads, landfills, old railroad beds and mine wastes, are infertile and support only scant vegetation. These are analogous to tephra of a variety of texture types early in primary succession. The substrates vary from fine ash to coarse scoria (loose gravel). We are no longer in a position to leave these places unattended near populated areas because such land is scarce, and must be rehabilitated effectively. Though many landforms are engineered in the initial stages of restoration, the ecological approach is better than

Fig. 3.5 Tree planting on Mt. Usu (Hokkaido, Japan). Many volunteers replant deep-rooted tree species to stabilize the tephra-coated slopes. By carefully selecting plant species and by organizing a phalanx of volunteers, thousands of plants can be installed in a few hours. These plants have high survival and grow rapidly to form woodlands in urban areas.

the commonly used agricultural approach, but requires the application of successional concepts and a long-term commitment to restoration.

Derelict urban sites are more fertile than mine wastes and are commonly infested with undesirable plants that can be used to indicate the required treatments at the site. Because this type of accidental vegetation does not support desirable wildlife and offers few amenities, it should be converted using methods appropriate to secondary succession. Rubble can be rehabilitated readily by the introduction of carefully selected species capable of outdoing ruderals. These species, usually trees and shrubs, might also attract birds, help cleanse the air and be more attractive to people in the neighborhood.

The difficulty of restoring vegetation on land mined for its sand is demonstrated by observations in sand and gravel quarries near Darwin, Australia. After 27 years, mined sites were poorly stocked, had many fewer species and were poorly developed compared with controls. Full recovery will take overt restoration efforts, but what these might be remains in question.

Fig. 3.6 Sod-covered houses in Iceland. Eleventh century farmhouses were dug into the turf and covered with thick roofs. These sturdy structures protected people and livestock during eruptions and were very snug and comfortable during the winter.

### 3.2.6   Interactions with other disturbances

Volcanoes often interact with glaciers. In Iceland, this strange juxtaposition of fire and ice has tempered the psyche of Icelanders. More than any other people, they know how distant volcanoes can cause devastating floods, and they have for centuries avoided building in dangerous habitats. Volcanoes such as Grímsvötn, erupting through huge continental glaciers, spawn massive flows of pumice to form *sandurs*, great black sand wastelands (see Section 3.4.2). Eleventh century farmhouses were embedded in the turf with thick sod roofs. Not only did these sturdy structures protect people and livestock during the long, harsh winters, but they also afforded protection from tephra that could fall without warning from the dark and cloudy sky (Fig. 3.6).

Voluminous rains, often associated with hurricanes, can trigger landslides on the steep slopes of dormant volcanoes. These landslides deposit debris, mud and boulders in their wake. A calm Mt. Rainier spawned such a lahar in 1947, when a debris dam broke, releasing a huge slurry down a small valley. This minor event helped to increase awareness of how quiescent volcanoes can interact with other forces of nature to produce catastrophes. A similar event had tragic consequences half a world away in 1953. A rubble dam on Mt. Ruapehu (New Zealand) broke, releasing a powerful lahar that weakened the Tangiwai Railway Bridge. When the overnight express passed over, the bridge collapsed, killing 151 people. Many devastating lahars have been spawned by heavy rain on unstable volcanic slopes, as for example on Mt. Pinatubo (1991). In 1998, Hurricane Mitch dumped a deluge of biblical proportions on Casita Volcano (Nicaragua) which spawned deadly avalanches. Unstable mountains also spawn lahars after earthquakes, as happened on Nevado del Huila (Colombia) in 1994. This lahar, down the Rio Paez, killed hundreds and destroyed several towns.

Volcanoes will continue to impact humanity with unpredictable, fierce eruptions. Little can be done except to increase the awareness of their danger, install warning systems where lahars are likely and attempt to relocate villages away from active volcanoes.

## 3.3  DUNES

### 3.3.1  Introduction

The atomic age began on the snow-white gypsum dunes near Alamogordo, New Mexico with the first nuclear explosion on July 16, 1945. That this wilderness was considered otherwise useless reveals much about how inland dunes were viewed. Today we realize that some dunes are valuable habitats that ought to be conserved. Dunes in many parts of the world support a unique biota that contributes to the tapestry of life. In Mozambique and in southern Queensland (Australia), dunes have developed for millennia. Young surfaces on the Cooloola Dunes along the Queensland (Australia) coast support scattered drought-tolerant shrubs and rhizomatous grasses (Fig. 3.7a). Eventually, after hundreds of years, stable dunes develop forest vegetation with a dense canopy and a sparse understory (Fig. 3.7b). As the canopy matures, an understory develops (Fig. 3.7c) and after millennia the forest is open, is dominated by large trees and has a diverse understory (Fig. 3.7d). After 100,000 years or more, most of the nutrients in the system are in the vegetation and the canopy is degenerating (Fig. 3.7e). The soil is extremely thin. Very old dunes, measured to have formed over 500,000 years ago, are clothed in stunted scrub, with low biomass, but very high biodiversity (Fig. 3.7f). Such ancient soils are devoid of nutrients and would make a poor choice for agriculture.

Many inland dunes are destructive. They march across continents, inexorably burying human habitats and smothering entire villages.

Fig. 3.7  Cooloola Dunes form along the central Queensland (Australia) coast. These sands can be dated precisely using optically stimulated luminescence. (a) Younger than 100 years: newly exposed sandy surfaces support only a few hardy shrubs and grasses. (b) 2,600 years: tree vegetation becomes well established, but the understory vegetation remains sparse. (c) 6,000 years: well-developed rainforest tree growth and some understory vegetation occur. (d) 50,000 years: the forest canopy is beginning to open, but large trees dominate, and the understory vegetation is well-developed. (e) 120,000 years: the forest canopy has begun to break up and the understory is dominated by heath species tolerant of the infertile conditions. (f) 500,000 years: the number of species reaches a peak, but the vegetation is stunted because the soil has been leached of virtually all nutrients.

Fig. 3.7 (cont.)

---

**Box 3.3  The Blood Rain**

In Sicily, they dread the Blood Rain (*La Pioggia di Sangue*). When
the dry North African sirocco meets moist northern air masses,
a muddy precipitation forms. Roger found that it coats cars,
porches, sidewalks and buildings with a dull rust-brown veneer that
keeps everyone busy cleaning windows, muttering and wondering
what further insults will occur that day. This wind-borne dust
results from overgrazing, desertification and erosion. While this
dust is a distinct nuisance, it adds nutrients to the landscape and
creates jobs for windshield washers.

---

These creeping disasters eliminate grazing lands and destroy the
livelihoods of millions of people. However, stabilized inland dunes can
also provide protection from wind and occasionally offer some recreation. Dunes are tied into large-scale geomorphic processes. They have
created productive land in the loess prairies of China and North
America, and winds that move inland dunes carry dust for thousands of
miles to enrich soils of such remote island systems as Hawaii. Dunes in
Africa produce fungal and bacterial diseases dust frequently causes
severe discomfort in Sicily and beyond (Box 3.3).

Coastal dunes, in contrast, are valuable barriers that protect
coastlines and homes from storms, provide recreation and enhance
biodiversity. Occasionally, coastal dunes move inland to bury forests,
but such occurrences usually occur after disturbances by humans.

Below, we discuss the importance of dunes and what we have learned from the study of natural stabilization processes. Can we stabilize inland dunes that threaten millions of people? Can we preserve coastal dunes that help to protect shorelines from hurricanes and tsunami? The answers will vary, of course, by location, but also with the will to seek efficient and comprehensive solutions.

### 3.3.2    Physical setting

Dunes are as varied as the landscapes that spawn them. To form a dune, winds in excess of 25 km per hour are needed. There must be a source of sand and the sand-bearing winds must then encounter some feature that deflects the wind and permits the sand to fall out. Sources of sand for inland dunes can result from dried lakes, eroding cliffs, glacial forelands or over-grazed lands. Dunes are part of a long-term cycle of sedimentation, rock formation, uplift into mountains, erosion and deposition into lakes and transport into dunes. Dunes eventually become buried and form part of the landscape. Eventually, they may be compressed into sandstone.

Throughout central Asia, as lakes dry up, massive dunes are created. Most inland dune systems are confined to arid regions, but some are near large lakes. They form where vegetation is limited and where there is enough wind to move sand. Almost by definition, inland sand dunes are mobile, dry and infertile. It is hard for plants to establish because growth rates rarely keep up with sand movements; inland dunes can resemble flowing mountains. Apparently stable, these dunes are actually quite dynamic. They erode from the upwind edges, and accumulate sand downwind. Even slowly moving dunes resist colonization due to local instability and the lack of local sources for plant invasion. Plants are usually confined to isolated, favorable sites and to the dune margins, so zonation is lacking. If the flow of an inland dune is halted, by a hill for example, then plants can begin to invade. Inland sand dunes have been expanding dramatically for over 100 years. During this period, and particularly in the last 30 years, global warming, increasing aridity, poor agricultural practices and expanding herds of livestock associated with burgeoning human populations have interacted to expose more land to erosion, desertification and the formation of mammoth sand dunes.

Coastal dunes form when eroding materials from reefs or cliffs interact with currents. Because the source of coastal dunes is sediments suspended in the ocean, and because the land rises away from the sea, zonation patterns are common. Zonation is sharp because dune morphology changes abruptly. Fore dunes brace the shore and are hostile environments for plants, so they rarely support more than a scattering of strand species common to the shore (Fig. 3.8). Though scattered hardy plants can be found that survive salt spray, being blasted by sand, periodic flooding by storm surges and chronically shifting sands, they do little to stabilize the fore dune. However, in some cases, tree species with seeds that are either wind-borne or waterborne can establish on the fore dune, as near Lake Michigan (Fig. 3.9) or on coral islands (Fig. 3.10), to initiate stabilization.

The leeward (inland) side of the first dune can be sufficiently stable to permit colonization, often by spreading grasses (Fig. 3.11). Between successive dunes, the dune slack occurs. These protected sites are moist and often sustain substantial vegetation, including wetlands that provide contrasting habitats and help to support wildlife (Fig. 3.12). Water tolerant species develop into mature vegetation, and persist unless they are overwhelmed by migrating dunes. Away from the shoreline, dunes may eventually develop extensive vegetation for several reasons. The surfaces are older and have accumulated organic matter, so fertility is greater and salt spray is reduced. Water holding

Fig. 3.8 Dune erosion in southern Oregon. Stabilized dunes can be undercut by waves and wind.

Fig. 3.9 Pioneer plants on Lake Michigan dunes (Indiana, USA). Woody species such as cottonwoods sometimes grow along the shore due to their excellent dispersal abilities.

Fig. 3.10 Dune stabilization on Heron Island in the Barrier Reef (Central Queensland, Australia). She-oaks (*Casuarina*) provide stabilization of small sand islands. *Banksia* and *Acacia* species are also common on such dunes.

Fig. 3.11  Dune stabilization on Fraser Island (Central Queensland, Australia). Rhizomatous grasses stabilize dunes and other unstable sandy habitats throughout the world.

Fig. 3.12  Dune slack lake along Lake Michigan (Indiana, USA). The dune slack adjacent to large lakes and many seashores often supports a shallow lake because impervious layers form to trap rainwater.

ability increases, nutrient inputs from wind augment fertility and the dune is invaded by species common to the uplands of the region.

Coastal dunes in southeast Queensland can develop into rain-forests given sufficient time. Although these dunes are initially infertile, they can sustain well-developed vegetation after several thousand years (Box 3.4; Fig 3.7). Typical sand dune succession starts with grasses and Nitrogen-fixing shrubs forming dense vegetation and then proceeds from open woodlands to closed forests that can be maintained for about 40,000 years. However, after that, when the aging landscape can no longer support the complex forests, retrogressive succession begins and the forest degenerates to a low woodland and heath. Nutrients are stored in standing plants and become unavailable in the litter. Of more importance is that nutrients are simply leached from the sand particles, restricting the nutrient pool to a very shallow layer. As Joe Walker has demonstrated, old landscapes cannot be expected to recover from disturbances in the ways that younger landscapes do.

### 3.3.3  Dunes in the lives of humans

Dunes symbolize deserts. From the true adventures of T. E. Lawrence (of Arabia) to the fictional planet *Dune*, the term connotes a harsh, shifting landscape where survival is always problematic and only the most adept survive. Dunes have conditioned the way cultures of many countries in Africa, the Middle East and central Asia respond to stress. They are embedded in the poetry and literature of semi-arid lands and were once, in ancient mindsets, equated to wilderness. Desertification, the rampant expansion of unproductive wastelands into range and pasture, is fueled by human population growth and accelerated by global warming. Overgrazing exposes the earth, and increasingly strong winds erode the surface to create dunes. This debilitating process poses an enormous challenge to many cultures. In affluent countries, inland dunes are less damaging and provide outlets for motorized recreation. They rarely cause overwhelming problems because the affected regions are marginal to the economies of richer countries. Yet in many places, where resources are scarce and no resource is too marginal to ignore, inland dunes are destroying the very fabric of life.

Tombouctou (Mali) is a threatened oasis, synonymous with the "ends of the earth." Expanding dunes of the Sahel surround this famous city. Once it was a center of culture and trade. Now, desert sands threaten to bury centuries-old mosques, and only continual removal of

---

**Box 3.4  Dunes in biodiversity**

Fraser Island, Queensland, a world heritage area, is the largest sand island in the world. Located just south of the Great Barrier Reef, this island is formed by sand deposited by currents. Roger and Lawrence have each explored the island. Over the millennia, dunes have stabilized and developed a diverse vegetation. Some have destabilized, forming "blowouts." The Dulinbara dune is encroaching the deep Lake Wabby and soon may fill it completely (Fig. 3.14). The diversity of vegetation is striking, and endemism is common. Grasses, morning glories and she-oaks slowly invade these infertile dunes. Open mixed woods dominated by eucalypts eventually develop. The nectar of banksia shrubs supports many species of birds. Near the crest of the island, stately forests dominate the ridges. Diversity is lower because many nutrients have been leached beyond the reach of roots of these species. In the swales, true rainforest occurs. Nutrients are recycled near the surface to maintain lush forests with trees as old as 1,200 years, and a wide variety of wildlife. Tree ferns, palms, strangler figs, vines, the majestic kauri and hoop pines form impressive forests. In the lee of the island, very old dunes have been leached of most nutrients, leading to woodland and scrub vegetation that is a remnant of once widespread vegetation on the mainland dunes. Along the immediate coast, periodic flooding leads to heath vegetation. Where sediments have been deposited, swamps dominated by mangroves form impenetrable barriers. These nutrient-rich habitats support a wide variety of sea birds and fauna. Fraser Island is a good place to explore dunes, lush rainforests and mangroves in a single day, if you dare to drive the narrow, rutted tracks.

---

the daily accumulation of sand protects the city. Only by constant maintenance and transport of the sand have the local people prevented the obliteration of these venerable, remarkable structures. The ever-present dunes of the Sahara have forged a tough, resilient people, but it is unclear how long human forces can keep the desert at bay.

Coastal dunes are viewed as a barrier to reaching a beach, or an object blocking the view. Thus, humans have been destroying coastal dunes at an alarming rate. Left intact, coastal dunes would protect lives and property. Coastal dunes can withstand the worst of storms and reduce the extent of tidal inundations.

### 3.3.4  Ecological responses

The concept of ecological succession developed from the study of dunes. Early ecologists in America and Europe outlined many principles of primary succession, and demonstrated the role of chance in determining the outcomes. The study of dunes has revealed many secrets about how vegetation develops.

Key to succession on dunes is stabilization. In nature, landforms usually arrest dune movement, though along coasts, dunes may stabilize simply because wind velocity drops away from the shoreline. Only a few species can start the stabilization, and grasses with deep and rapidly spreading root systems are the most common stabilizers. The first species establish precariously in particularly favorable micro-sites, and then expand. Because seedlings can rarely grow fast enough to get roots down to stable, moist layers, plants that spread by vegetative means predominate. Grasses with strongly spreading rhizomes can also spread into dunes from the edges and accelerate stabilization. Other pioneers have prostrate stems that form interlocking systems. In many cases, N-fixing species soon follow to accelerate what is called "facilitation," where plants improve local growing conditions (see Section 3.4). Lupines and pea-vines are common N-fixing, herbaceous invaders of dunes, while several shrubs (e.g. wax-myrtle, buckthorn) also fix nitrogen and can invade dunes.

Once stabilized, a few more species can establish and vegetation can start to develop. For a seed to germinate and mature, it must find a "safe-site." Often the safe-site can be recognized by its physical features such as a small depression, a patch of stable sand or proximity to a larger plant. In other cases, the particular attribute that characterizes a safe-site is subtle. Slightly more favorable water levels or more nitrogen may be crucial, but difficult to detect by instrumentation. The germinating seedling does, however, experience the difference. Early in succession, a safe-site can support most of the species reaching it, so that a strong element of chance comes into play. Where moss crusts form, small-seeded plants can establish by rooting in small crevices, protected from desiccation by the moss. Later in succession, suitable conditions become more customized to individual species, and species turnover may occur due to competition. Still later, safe-sites become rare because competition from adult plants overrides potential benefits of particular microsites.

As vegetation develops, it follows trajectories. Traditional ecologists viewed trajectories as predictable, always leading to the same type of vegetation, called a "climax" community. This process involves convergence from different initial communities and precludes variations in final species composition. Very few studies on dunes have demonstrated convergence. When comparing trajectories, there are two other alternatives: divergence or parallel development. The vegetation of two nearly identical sites may diverge over time because the effects of small initial differences are magnified. If different species colonize each site by chance, and if these species alter the site in different ways, then subsequent colonizing species will be different, leading to divergence in the eventual vegetation. Alternatively, initial differences may be unchanged, because the physical environment precludes the biota from reducing the variation among sites. With this scenario, two different dunes may develop on parallel yet distinct trajectories. A series of sites may display elements of each of these conditions, resulting in a complex network of trajectories, and ultimately a mosaic of vegetation.

The practical result is that predicting the outcome for a particular site is difficult. There are several alternative results, each of which could potentially serve as a model for restoration. When exotic species invade, a novel pattern of development, called deflected succession, may occur. The introduction of lupines to coastal dunes in northern California has created new stable assemblages. It is also possible that species found early in the trajectory can suppress invasion, leading to arrested succession.

Cryptobiotic crusts can form when dunes stabilize, but the process is very slow. Moss crusts may take 250 years to develop in the southwestern USA. Photosynthetic bacteria are prominent components of these crusts, so that as carbon is accumulated, fertility begins to improve and seedlings can establish. In the absence of further disturbance, the dune can be stabilized. Old, stable dunes are common in parts of the southwestern USA, where it is sometimes difficult to determine that the vegetation is underlain by dunes produced a few thousand years ago. Unfortunately, crusts are very sensitive to trampling, grazing or vehicular traffic, so under the current, intensive grazing regimes their role in dune stabilization is limited.

Due to the unpredictable introduction of dominant species, disturbances and chance, dunes, like other primary sites, will undergo a long phase where vegetation forms a mosaic of contrasting types. Examples of dune slack vegetation in several parts of the world demonstrate how identical habitats can support different vegetation. Vegetation on old stable dunes can retain its identities for thousands of years without succession. A mosaic therefore consists of multiple stable states, all of which have equal claim to being normal, climax vegetation.

### 3.3.5  Human responses

The failure to respond to encroaching dunes has global implications. We ignore them at our peril. The Sumerians, who provided the wellspring of western civilization, lived in the rich valleys of the Tigris and Euphrates rivers. The culture that developed a writing system and invented the wheel today inhabits a land of dust storms and deserts, an object lesson in desertification. Desertification affects over one-third of the earth's land and over one billion people. Dunes in the Amu Darya Valley of Afghanistan cover 300 by 30 km (about the size of Lebanon). They advance a meter per day and have engulfed over 100 villages in the last decade, smothering oases used for millennia. China is seeing its deserts merge into massive conglomerates. An area of Nigeria equal to the size of Gambia is being covered annually. Coping with desertification is a huge job that will require greatly improved land management to ameliorate the effects of grinding poverty. Ecologically informed revegetation is but the first step in this process. The costs of rehabilitation and reduced desertification will be much smaller than the costs of letting the sands blow unchecked.

The challenge of this first step to push back the desert is huge. Dunes require human intervention in order to be restored. They must be stabilized if they are blowing away or smothering inland vegetation, but stabilization is retarded because plants usually fail to establish root systems before they succumb to the shifting substrate. Stabilization is further complicated by societal impediments. Materials used to stabilize a dune often disappear to be used for fuel, or sold on a black market to obtain desperately needed cash. Timely stabilization of inland desert dunes and restoration of buried lands to productive states are major challenges that will involve social and political as well as ecological approaches.

Many tactics for dune stabilization have been applied successfully. Physical barriers such as fences can slow movement. Biodegradable mesh pads can be laid down to facilitate crust formation and seedling establishment. Once stabilized, rhizomatous grasses can be planted, as long as they can be cared for until well established. Where it is crucial to stabilize a dune with vegetation, low levels of fertilization may be applied, but only after trials confirm the appropriate amounts.

Too much fertilization will favor exotic, aggressive species. Exotic species can be removed manually in some cases. When the exotic is an N-fixing species, the challenge is great (Box 3.5). Rehabilitation of dunes should include a variety of species as insurance against subsequent disturbance. Current best practices for coastal dune restoration emphasize low fences and planting of a very restricted number of species. We encourage practitioners to explore the use of a wider spectrum of species.

Relict dunes sometimes underlie stunted, struggling vegetation. These old dunes are not suited to agriculture, though attempts have been made to develop pastures or crops. Vegetation on these dunes can be improved and incorporated into pastoral landscapes. Care must be taken in the management of dunes to balance fertility levels, eliminate or control invasive plants and plan for only modest grazing. Knowing how dune vegetation develops can improve the productivity and utility of wide sections of semi-arid lands.

While desert dunes are a natural result of large-scale geological processes, humans have accelerated the rate at which dunes form and migrate. Forestalling desertification, of course, would have been the best way to deal with desert dunes. Dune stabilization is one of several approaches needed to arrest and roll back desertification. It appears to be among the greatest of all land use challenges for humanity.

The Chinese government is fully aware of its problems with desertification and has tried many approaches to dune stabilization. One promising method is to plant trees and grasses in a checkerboard pattern to arrest dune formation. The Chinese government reports major reductions in the buildup of dunes and an increase of forest cover. During the 1970s and 1980s, a system of agricultural "shelterbelts" was implemented by reforesting large tracts of land to anchor and irrigate loose soil and to help stem the flow of dust storms across China.

Dunes can be sapped of their strength by eliminating or denying their source of sand. Long series of sand traps can be installed upwind of dunes, so that while the dune continues to erode from its leading edge, it is not replenished. Dunes then disappear by attrition. While this is a long-term solution, it can work, particularly if erosion is accelerated mechanically, for example by dragging chains across the landforms. As the dune shrinks to a manageable size, it can be stabilized and its fertility enhanced using combinations of binding plants and nitrogen-fixing plants. Because biological conservation is a low priority, growing almost anything to stabilize "disaster" dunes is acceptable. It is likely

---

**Box 3.5  A success story**

The Lanphere Dunes, Humboldt Bay National Wildlife Refuge, form a nearly pristine coastal dune complex that is the largest of its kind along the Pacific Coast. These dunes are the last vestiges of those that once dominated much of coastal California. Restoration has focused on both habitats and species. The native dune grass, once so common, is now confined to only two California localities. Several other uncommon species occur (Humboldt Bay wallflower, beach layia, pink sand-verbena). These dunes, along with most others along the Pacific Coast of North America, were invaded by European beach grass. Its dominance significantly alters physical dune characteristics, including sand transport mechanisms, and stresses native plant communities.

Andrea Pickart led a team that rehabilitated these dunes in a 4 ha area, manually removing the European beach grass. This required about 15 return visits to remove sprouts, but after two years native cover and composition had recovered. Such a low-tech approach can be exported to many places and can be adapted to implementation by volunteers.

---

that such reclaimed land would be grazed, so a mixture of unpalatable species (to prevent erosion) and palatable species should be used.

Where stable dunes provide biological and recreational values (e.g. White Sands USA and the Karoo Desert of South Africa), their protection and rehabilitation have high priority. Methods used for coastal dunes apply to the stabilization of desert dunes. Minimizing physical impacts, stabilizing "blowouts" (Fig. 3.13; Fig. 3.14), planting stabilizing species and providing maintenance care form part of the comprehensive plan for recovering dune qualities.

Current approaches to dealing with desert dunes are based on agricultural or forestry models combined with efforts to reduce sand movement by mechanical means. Only a limited amount of ecological information is being applied, and the scale of the problem often overwhelms the available resources. Dune stabilization and restoration programs continue to be slow. Yet human impacts are causing damage at accelerating rates, so better restoration methods must be developed. Ways to improve establishment, for example by early protection from herbivory or the creation of safe-sites, should be fully explored.

Fig. 3.13 Dune invasion of forest on the shores of Lake Michigan (Indiana, USA). Disturbance can destroy the stability of a dune. Here dunes have overwhelmed a deciduous forest.

Fig. 3.14 Dune destruction of Lake Wabby on Fraser Island (Central Queensland coast, Australia). One of many perched on the world's longest sand island, this lake is being buried by sands borne on winds blowing off the Coral Sea.

Humans need to act now to put the "marching deserts" described by Paul Sears (in 1935!) on the retreat. Coordinated programs to arrest dune expansion, reduce soil erosion and redirect development funds to support affected populations in more sustainable ways must be found and put into place.

### 3.3.6   Interactions with other disturbances

Inland dunes are driven by strong winds and are concentrated in arid regions remote from summer monsoons. Dunes are more common in regions with extensive sandstone mountains, which provide sand sources, and where high atmospheric pressure predominates, limiting rainfall. Disturbances that disrupt vegetation increase soil erosion and accelerate dune formation. Overgrazing, off-road recreational vehicles and firewood collection are such disturbances. Recent development activities have allowed deep drilling for wells to support livestock. These actions have led to local denudation, expansion of pastoral herds, further erosion and lowering of the water table. These combine to accelerate dune formation. The increase in dunes covering the landscape is most closely linked to the expansion of pastoral herds. Therefore, a major component to stabilizing and rehabilitating dunes will be to achieve sustainable levels in the numbers of grazing animals and reduce the numbers and extent of feral populations.

### 3.4   GLACIERS

### 3.4.1   Introduction

Glaciers have greatly affected past human activities, modify our current distribution on this planet, provide the largest reservoir of fresh water and will be critical to our survival. With most of the world's glaciers melting, frozen corpses are emerging to reveal details about human history and vast new areas are being exposed for colonization by plants, animals and perhaps people (Box 3.6). Decreasing ocean salinity may alter global climates and increasing sea levels will displace many urban residents. In this section, we explore the importance of glaciers to humans on global and local scales. What lessons does post-glacial succession have for modern restoration?

---

**Box 3.6  The ice gives back its victims**

In 1991, a frozen corpse of a man, nicknamed Ötzi the Iceman, who had been dead for more than 5,300 years was found at 3,200 m on an alpine glacier in Italy. In the well-preserved pouch he carried, on his clothing and in his stomach, scientists found many plant species, probably used for food and medicine. This kind of record helps us trace human interactions with a changing environment. The man froze after being shot in the shoulder with an arrow during a period slightly warmer than the twentieth century. Then the climate cooled and preserved his corpse. Now it is warming again and the alpine glacier that once held him is melting. Glaciers throughout the world are spewing out mammoths, lost climbers and the remains of long-dead vegetation.

---

### 3.4.2  Physical setting

Glaciers cover 10 percent of the earth's surface today, with 95 percent of that cover in Greenland and Antarctica. Glaciers have advanced and retreated across the earth's surface many times during its history due to the movement of the earth's crust (plate tectonics) and the changing shape of its orbit around the sun. In the last 600 million years, there have been only three glacial ages, or periods when warm tropical ocean water was restricted from mixing with the colder polar water and ice covered at least one of the poles. One glacial age began 450 million(M) years before the present (BP). Another began 350M BP. The latest began just 2M BP, triggered by the closing of the Isthmus of Panama that sent the moisture-rich Gulf Stream northward and perhaps by the rise of the Himalayan Mountains that have, in turn, directed more moist air to the north.

Both poles are now ice-covered, in part because a landmass (Antarctica) covers the South Pole and the Arctic Ocean is isolated from warmer oceans. When the crustal plates are aligned to favor glacial ages, other forces create so-called Milankovich cycles of glacial advances of about 100,000 years duration followed by interglacial retreats of about 10,000 years. These forces involve the shape of earth's orbit around the sun and its tilt relative to the sun. Interglacial periods occur when northern hemisphere summers are closest to the sun, increasing ice melt. During the last one million years there have been eight glacial advances, each followed by an interglacial, in which glaciers retreat poleward. We are now at the end of an interglacial, following a maximum advance of ice about 18K (thousand) BP. Presumably, were it not for human activities, the earth would now cool and we would enter another glacial epoch. This may be delayed as much as 1,000 years, however, by human-induced global warming. In fact, one recent suggestion is that early human agricultural activities during the last several thousand years have produced enough carbon dioxide (from cutting forests) and methane (from cultivating rice in flooded fields and promoting livestock populations) to forestall the predicted cooling.

Glaciers shape the land in remarkable ways. When ice reaches about 60 m depth, the lower surfaces become plastic and the whole ice mass moves like a slow stream down slope. Then the ice picks up soil and rocks, and acts as a giant sander, effectively flattening continents. In the mountains, glaciers carve new landforms and accentuate the topography. In northern North America, ice-free refugia (nunataks) were common along coastal areas and on the tops of very tall mountains 18K BP, but everything else was submerged under several kilometers of ice.

The melting of the ice reveals smashed mountain ranges, new, U-shaped valleys and many local phenomena (Fig. 3.15). *Rouches moutonnées*, or stone sheep, are glacially carved hills that have a gradual slope from north that ends in a steep south-facing cliff in Northern Hemisphere. As the ice carved higher on the rock, pressure increased, forcing water into cracks in the hill. Freezing of this water then resulted in the plucking of rock chunks from the southern side of hill. Another feature of glaciated landscapes is a *monadnock* or isolated hill of erosion-resistant rock. A classic example is Mt. Monadnock in southern New Hampshire, USA.

When the Laurentide ice sheet in North America melted, enormous changes occurred. Large lakes formed in front of glaciers where drainage was blocked by ice or debris. When the ice melted, long spillways or *coulees* formed. Another rapid melting of ice occurs when volcanoes erupt under glaciers. Both of these forms of massive floods or *jökulhlaups* can create sandur (broad, sandy outwash plains) when the flow is not confined to a narrow valley. Formed by extensive sheet flow and characterized by many ill-defined, braided drainage channels on a slightly inclined landscape, sandur are prominent features immediately downstream of glaciers at high latitudes (Svalbard, Iceland, Greenland, Canada, Alaska and Siberia). Historically, glacial melting created sandur in the Great Plains of North America, Jutland in Denmark and the Canterbury Plains of New

Fig. 3.15 The Emmons Glacier on Mt. Rainier (Washington, USA) is in full retreat. It was down this valley that the Osceola lahar swept about 5,600 years ago.

Zealand. Sandur also occur under the ocean and perhaps even on Mars. A dramatic jökulhlaup occurred in November 1996 in southern Iceland when a volcanic eruption under the Vatnajökull ice cap melted $3\,km^3$ of glacial ice. Initially contained in a sub-glacial reservoir, this heated water eventually broke out and dumped about 180 million tons of sediment across an area of $750\,km^2$ (the size of Tonga). Over $7\,km^2$ of new land was added along the shore. At its peak, the discharge became the second largest river in the world ($50,000$ $m^3$ per second). Several bridges were destroyed but no lives were lost in the sparsely inhabited area. Damage was modest, but significant.

Lateral, central and terminal moraines develop where rocks carried by the ice are deposited. These moraines may reach tens of meters in elevation and determine future drainage and colonization patterns. Chunks of remnant ice melt to form kettle holes, depressions that can fill with water and provide safe-sites. Glacial sediments or till range from very fine silts (or rock flour) to large boulders and are washed downhill to fill in other depressions in a complete reworking of the landscape. Dry, cold winds off the ice sheet can pick up finer particles and create dunes.

Box 3.7  Kayaking where glaciers recently stood

Over five days, Lawrence paddled his kayak past three glaciers, dozens of bears, 80 years of history, thousands of alder trees and millions of mosquitoes. During his visit just 13 years ago to Glacier Bay National Park in southeast Alaska, these glaciers met the salt water in wide walls of ice. Now the ice has melted back to expose sands, gravels and larger rocks that had been buried under the ice for thousands of years (Fig. 3.16; Fig. 3.17). Just 80 years ago, his whole trip would have been by skis and crampons on a gigantic ice field. Now it is by kayak on the water.

In Glacier Bay, Alaska, USA, the youngest sites, just free of ice, are a primal collage of rushing streams, eroding slopes and exposing rocky barrens that make up a constantly changing surface (Box 3.7). Older forelands are flatter, with meandering streams that emerge from the bottom of the crumbling, often dirty wall of ice and gently rearrange the fine silts. In alpine areas, a melting glacier results in a constantly eroding cliff face or landslide, with rocks loosened from the ice crashing down the slopes (Fig. 3.16, Fig. 3.17). A photogenic wall of ice is most common when a glacier is advancing.

### 3.4.3   Glaciers in the lives of humans

We find ourselves in rather unusual circumstances — a rare inter-glacial period within a rare glacial age. In fact, the rise of agriculture and modern human society may be largely due to the relatively favorable climatic conditions we are experiencing. The retreating ice has dramatically affected human evolution, culture, diet and survival. Clothing and tools in the northern hemisphere evolved in a peri-glacial environment. Certainly, human history has been intimately intertwined with glaciers. Extensive glaciation leads to lowered ocean levels and oceans may have been as much as 80–120 m below current levels about 18K BP. The exposure of continental shelves facilitated human migrations to North America across the Bering Strait and the coloni-zation of newly exposed islands around the world. Where mountain ranges go north to south, as in North America, people, plants and animals migrated ahead of the advancing ice, and then back as the ice melted. In Europe, migration was impeded by the Alps, which go east to west. A relatively warm period starting about 6K BP (the Hypsithermal or Flandrian period) allowed colonization of northern

Fig. 3.16  Muir Glacier (Glacier Bay, Alaska) in 1983. Note the full wall of ice remaining from this tidewater glacier that had melted back 100 km from the ocean during the previous 200 years (Box 3.7).

Fig. 3.17  Muir Glacier (Glacier Bay, Alaska) in 1999. Since 1983 (Fig. 3.16), this tidewater glacier had lost its wall of ice and is completely grounded (Box 3.7).

Europe. Temperatures remained warm enough for the colonization of Iceland and Greenland about 1K BP. However, the return of colder climates, culminating in the Little Ice Age about AD 1350−1860, resulted in loss of farms, villages and even the whole isolated

Fig. 3.18 Drangajökull Glacier (northwestern Iceland). A small remnant ice bridge is all that remains of the face of this glacier in Iceland, suggesting that global warming is accelerating.

European population of Greenland that gradually lost contact with Iceland. Reliant on agriculture and imports of food and tools from Europe, the Norse in Greenland gradually became stunted from malnutrition, and died off. Since about AD 1860, glaciers have been retreating around the world (Fig. 3.18; Fig. 3.19). Today, outside of polar regions, most glaciers are limited to tall mountain ranges and do not directly impact an increasingly urbanized human population. Glaciers are often seen as benign examples of huge, ponderous natural forces and are most often visited in a relatively pristine, wilderness landscape. Yet the indirect implications of glaciers on humans are enormous.

Glaciers provide fascinating environments for researchers examining life under harsh conditions. In Greenland, glaciers provide impressive records of historical concentrations of gases such as carbon dioxide, helping to reveal climate change during the last 110,000 years. Of course, glaciers are also dangerous. When advancing glaciers (or moraines from retreating glaciers) block fjords or rivers, lakes can form that frequently drain suddenly in catastrophic jökulhlaups (glacier outburst floods). Such floods can endanger animals and people living within the flood zone. Recent examples come from Iceland, Alaska,

Fig. 3.19  Glacial foreland of Franz Josef Glacier (New Zealand).
The newly exposed surface in front of a glacier is very unstable and
generally inhospitable to plant growth.

British Columbia and Peru, but historical jökulhlaups helped shape
much of the topography of glaciated continents. Perhaps the most
bizarre human interaction with glaciers is the plan to haul icebergs
from polar regions to thirsty tropical lands.

With global warming comes the acceleration of the melting of the
world's glaciers. Thirty-two percent of the 100 million km$^3$ of ice occurs
as glaciers in Antarctica and Greenland. In Antarctica, several huge ice
sheets have broken off ice shelves in the last five years and many glaciers
that reach the ocean have been retreating at an average rate of 50 m per
year since 1950. One monster iceberg (B-15A) is 115 km long, has an area
over 2,500 km$^2$ (the size of Luxembourg) and broke off from the Ross Ice
Shelf in March 2000. Since then, it has drifted into McMurdo Sound. This
makes access to McMurdo Station difficult and extends the trek
penguins must make to the open ocean. This enormous mass of ice
has calved 15 other icebergs without losing its enormous size. While
ocean currents, wind and precipitation patterns and several other

factors influence this glacial melting, recent global warming caused by human activities is probably an important cause.

Glaciers in Greenland are melting faster than previously realized, dumping 167 km$^3$ of ice into the Atlantic Ocean in 2005 either directly from meltwater or from ice cracking off the ends of the glaciers where they meet the ocean. This represents a 57 percent increase in ice loss over 1996 levels. Surface meltwaters, identifiable as big blue pools when one flies over Greenland, have seeped under the glaciers, lubricating and speeding their flow. Greenland's ice sheet encompasses 1.7 million km$^2$ (the size of Iran) at depths of up to 3 km and the meltwater from 2005 alone would supply the entire city of New York with enough fresh water for 115 years.

Arctic sea ice has decreased from 7.5 million km$^2$ in 1980 to 5.5 million km$^2$ in 2005 (a decrease equal to the area of Mexico), and icebreakers are now having a relatively easy time traversing the North Pole. Increasing cloudiness, perhaps from increased humidity above the melting ice, may have slowed the rate of ice melt, but at the current rate the ice cap at the North Pole may be gone in 30 years. The darker ocean absorbs more heat than the white ice, so ocean temperatures may be expected to increase even more.

The most dramatic melting is occurring on alpine glaciers, particularly those in the tropics. On Mt. Kilimanjaro, Tanzania, a tropical alpine glacier has persisted for 11,000 years but may disappear by 2020. Most tropical alpine glaciers are found in South America where many have lost two-thirds of their volume in the last 15 years. However, the problem is global. Glacier National Park, Montana, USA may need to be renamed, as its glaciers are disappearing. West Meren Glacier in New Guinea disappeared in the late 1990s. Mt. Kenya has lost seven of its 18 glaciers since 1900. Many of these alpine glaciers began receding long before humans accelerated the naturally occurring warming trend, though there are some glaciers in places like western Norway and on Mt. Shasta, USA that are growing. Nevertheless, globally there is no doubt that the extent and rate of glacial melting is increasing and largely driven by human impacts on global warming.

There are many consequences of losing glaciers. Most importantly, glacial melt will contribute to raising ocean levels. The melting of the ice contained in all the mountain glaciers in the world would increase ocean levels by about 23 cm, a possibility by the year 2100. Add to this a meltdown of Greenland and the Antarctic ice caps and oceans could cause ocean levels to rise more than a meter. In contrast, oceans have risen only 15 cm in the last 100 years. Simultaneous thermal expansion would cause ocean levels to rise even more. This rise is a huge problem because 20 percent of us live within 30 km of the coast. Already Bangladesh is experiencing major difficulties and villagers on coral islands in the southwestern Pacific Ocean are being relocated. The melting of mountain glaciers can lead to initial flooding followed by drought, as water is no longer stored in its frozen state.

Potentially the greatest impact of glacial melting would be if the addition of so much fresh water into the North Atlantic were to stop the cycling of ocean water. The sinking of heavy, salty water at the north end of the Gulf Stream near Norway provides a pumping mechanism that is believed to pull water from the southern Atlantic and even the Indian Ocean. If this sinking were stopped because fresh water is lighter than salt water, the North Atlantic might cool drastically because the Gulf Stream waters no longer warm the area. There is recent evidence that the volume of warm water flowing north via the Gulf Stream is already declining, much faster than was predicted. The larger implications of the halting of the cycling of Atlantic waters are unknown but would probably impact every country bordering the Atlantic and Indian Oceans, altering precipitation and climate in unforeseen ways. Finally, huge shifts in the masses of water in glaciers and oceans may increase tectonic activity throughout the world.

Glacial melting is not all negative. Large surface areas are becoming exposed for potential exploitation for agriculture, forestry, recreation or ecological studies (e.g. of colonization and succession). As the local hydrology and climate change, wildlife and plants will be impacted and some species ranges will expand. In addition, the exposure of human remains by melting glaciers in Europe, North and South America has given archaeologists a chance to interpret past human migrations, cultures and diets. These individuals have been given colorful names such as Ötzi the Iceman, Inca Ice Maiden and Long Ago Man Found. The Tlingit Indians of southeastern Alaska have orally transmitted traditions that their people used Glacier Bay for hunting and fishing through several cycles of glacial advance and retreat. Now, with much of the bay exposed by recent glacial retreats, the Tlingit people are trying to negotiate future subsistence uses of the bay that is now Glacier Bay National Park.

Melting ice also influences shipping and tourism. Ocean shipping, that moves 90 percent of all goods around the world, will have routes directly across the Arctic Ocean, reducing time and costs of transport. Tourism will also need to adapt to changing conditions. For example, ski areas in Europe have to build snow bridges from their lifts to the snow-capped glaciers, and ski areas in many countries are relying increasingly on man-made snow. Marginal ski areas will simply have to close. Thousands of tourists ogle tidewater glaciers from cruise ships in Alaska, drive to accessible glaciers near highways in Iceland and New Zealand, or walk to the base of, climb or even fly up onto the ice (as at Franz Josef Glacier). In Iceland, snow vehicles take people for rides on Europe's largest glacier. The pristine ice surfaces of Antarctica are becoming the latest tourist rage. Ironically, as glacier-related tourism grows, glaciers shrink in the face of global warming.

### 3.4.4   Ecological responses

Glacial retreats provide excellent laboratories to study succession and to develop strategies to restore similar, man-made habitats. Good, direct observations of glacial retreats during the last few hundred years provide dates for when each portion of the moraine was exposed. Older dates can be determined by lichen growth on moraines, historical literature such as the Icelandic Sagas and by the dating of organic remains such as tree trunks (and humans!) that were trapped under the advancing ice.

The retreat of a coastal glacier may leave behind a fjord when the ocean fills an ice-carved valley. Tidewater glaciers are most stable when they rest on the bottom of the sea, such as on a terminal moraine that the glacier itself produced. However, ice that is floating without support often melts very quickly, as in Glacier Bay, Alaska where a network of several hundred kilometers of fjord was exposed in the last 200 years. Terrestrial glaciers melt back leaving forelands full of the physical features described above. For plants, such unstable terrain often resembles a moonscape and is difficult to colonize.

The glacial foreland is not as sterile as a volcanic surface, but it is not particularly fertile, either, especially where there is exposed bedrock that has been scraped bare by ice. However, plants and animals can survive, and soils can even develop on, in or under the ice. Small forests can even develop on the ice when soil falls onto a glacier from an adjacent landslide. Yet, most organisms that survive are small and short-lived, such as algae that live in the ice itself.

Most plants, animals and microorganisms arrive only after the ice melts, brought by birds, wind or water from the surrounding landscape. In protected areas, dust, plant matter and windblown insects gather and, with the aid of microorganisms, soil formation begins. Within just a few years, the soils in front of glaciers are teeming with soil microbes. The first plant colonists often establish along waterways that drain the new terrain or in areas adjacent to kettle ponds. The distribution of stable surfaces and adequate moisture can determine the location of early plant growth, and thus affect all subsequent colonization. Even if a pond dries up later, the signature of its former presence in the landscape might be evident from the lowered level of the soil surface or the shape and species composition of the plants growing in the old pond site.

In the standard textbook description of succession on barren rocks, succession starts with lichens, and is followed by mosses, herbs and finally woody plants. While this is sometimes true, often it is not. This view of primary succession, that each life form represents a successional stage that is necessary to "prepare the way" for the next stage, is called the relay floristics model. It is almost 100 years old. It emphasizes the positive influences of early successional species on later arrivals and so it is also called the facilitation model. Another model, almost as old, is called initial floristics composition (IFC). IFC emphasizes that seeds and spores of many different species of plants may arrive early in succession but they grow at different rates and different sizes, so that succession as we perceive it is merely a sequence of relative conspicuousness. In other words, shrub and tree seedlings may exist under the dense herbs and grasses in early stages, but we do not see them until they emerge years later, growing more slowly but to a greater final size. Both relay floristics and IFC are too simple to explain the real world. Besides the positive influence of one species on subsequent ones (relay floristics) or the lack of influence (IFC), one can imagine a scenario where the early colonists slow down or inhibit later colonists. This competitive inhibition model (or CI) states that whichever species gets to a site first dominates the resources. In both primary and secondary succession, any two species may have positive, negative or no influences on each other at different times during their lives and under different environmental conditions. The excitement in successional studies now is to sort out the relative importance of these various interactions in different areas of the world, on different substrates and across gradients of resources such as light and nutrients.

On glacial moraines, the pattern of succession depends on whether the glacier is at 5,000 m elevation on a tropical mountain, at sea level along a polar coast, or somewhere between. In other words, what plants (and the animals likely to carry those plants) are closest to the glacial moraine? Some well-dispersed plants, such as common grasses, are likely on many moraines, but most plants are specific to a given climate and biome or vegetation type. The surface or substrate also impacts post-glacial succession. On smooth, dry granite surfaces, lichens may indeed dominate for decades, followed by mosses and herbs, then bushes like blueberry and acid-tolerant trees like pines and oaks. This pattern follows relay floristics, where each stage makes the environment more suited for later stages. Lichens, that symbiosis between algae or cyanobacteria and fungi, are successful as pioneers under these harsh conditions. They can survive desiccation for years and can either fix nitrogen or obtain it from rainwater. In contrast, on a mostly smooth surface with lots of cracks, shrubs or trees can be the first colonizers on bare rock because they are capable of sending long roots down into the accumulating debris collecting in the cracks. On glacial silts or peri-glacial dunes, grasses might be the best colonizers, as they can rapidly send out multiple horizontal stems or stolons that stabilize the surface and maximize nutrient and water absorption. Generalizations about primary succession on post-glacial surfaces are therefore exceedingly difficult, but this wealth of patterns helps us to relate post-glacial surfaces to certain human-created surfaces.

Nitrogen levels are initially low, so organisms that fix atmo-spheric nitrogen into forms available to plants have an advantage (Plate 5). Free-living cyanobacteria fix nitrogen and frequently form dense gelatinous mats in early successional ponds but they also can live in the soil or on the surface of the ground. Bacteria that fix nitrogen and live inside roots of larger plants may help give such plants an advantage over other plants lacking that capability. Lupines are typical colonists of glacial moraines in Alaska and British Columbia, as they are on other infertile substrates. A robust species of lupine was introduced to Iceland about 40 years ago in order to stabilize eroding soils on glacial moraines and lava fields and has now become a widespread invasive of newly exposed floodplains.

Another bacterium that looks like strands of fungi and fixes nitrogen infects about 20 genera of plants in a variety of families. These plants are mostly woody (legumes can be herbaceous or woody) and often occur early in primary succession but not often as the initial colonists. It appears that plants infected with nitrogen-fixing bacteria need a certain level of soil carbon and soil nitrogen present in order to begin the energetically expensive process of nitrogen fixation. Such soil development often occurs slowly as small, herbaceous plants grow and die. However, once a woody plant with nitrogen-fixing bacteria such as alder (common on floodplains and glacial moraines throughout the northern hemisphere) or faya tree (*Myrica faya*, common on some volcanic islands in the subtropics) becomes established, soil nitrogen levels increase rapidly. Sometimes these woody plants with the nitrogen-fixing symbionts aid and sometimes they inhibit the establishment and growth of later successional trees. The relationship appears to be linked to how fertile the site is initially. Where the soil is rather infertile, the nitrogen can facilitate the growth of later successional species, while in fertile habitats the nitrogen-fixer gives no special advantage to later successional species. In fact, nitrogen-fixing species may be less dominant here than at sites where fertility is low.

Several studies to detail the importance of nitrogen to succession have been conducted on glacial moraines. However, no thorough study of succession on glacial moraines has been conducted across fertility gradients. Complicating the understanding of naturally occurring nitrogen accumulation in primary succession are both the rapid spread of weeds with nitrogen-fixing symbionts and air and ground additions of nitrogen from fertilizers and ammonia and nitrous oxides from air pollution.

Other nutrients required for plant growth are often present in the silts left from the glacier, at least in quantities sufficient to support early plant development. Over much longer stretches of time than the typical 500-year perspective for most studies of succession, phosphorus and other nutrients are often depleted in primary succession soils. Studies are underway to examine why these losses occur.

### 3.4.5   Human responses

Studies of primary succession on glacial moraines have many implications for society and for restoration. Continental glaciers once covered much of northern North America, Europe and Asia. Alpine glaciers dominated many contemporary mountain ranges as they still do only in the Himalayas. Therefore, much of the vegetation of these areas is due to post-glacial succession. Knowing just what to restore disturbed lands to is partly a matter of looking around at what grows there today.

In North America, Europe and Asia, species migrated north (or expanded from ice-free refuges) after the melting glaciers. Those species that could travel most rapidly now dominate the northern forests of the world. Wind pollination and light, wind-blown seeds favor rapid migration. Birches and willows probably dominated the early periglacial landscapes. Oaks, maples and hickories followed with heavier seeds. Today, pines and spruces dominate the boreal forest, species that are wind pollinated but have relatively heavy seeds. These trees are adapted, however, to the cold winters and hot summers of the north by their evergreen nature and tolerance of low-nutrient, often waterlogged soils. Although dispersal is important, so is adaptation to local weather and soil conditions.

Another lesson from the past comes from nunataks. Within the vast stretches of ice, there were pockets where some plants and animals survived. These areas were mostly along coastal mountain ranges, such as in Canada and Norway, but occasionally on mountain-tops not covered by ice. The importance of these species to the maintenance of species diversity in post-glacial colonization is not fully understood, but their survival points to the importance of con-sidering legacy effects in reconstructing ecosystems today. Combined with those organisms that resided in, on or under the ice, these survivors were certainly critical in influencing primary succession. As we have seen, glacial moraines are not initially sterile. Only volcanoes and some human-caused disturbances such as pavement or mine tailings produce lifeless conditions, and then only for a short while after the surface is formed. Restoration then becomes a matter of combining new species with those already there. Failure to incorporate the influence of the survivors does not advance the goals of restoration.

The surfaces left by glaciers vary, as we have noted, from steep escarpments, to rounded moraines, to nearly flat outwash plains. Analogous human disturbances include gravel pads, roadside verges and mine tailings, where terrain much reworked by dredges or bulldozers is often left compacted with many ridges and steep edges. Rocky shorelines exposed in lake drawdown zones can also resemble glacial moraines. Many construction sites leave similar gravel pads and reworked areas. During the construction of the Alaska oil pipeline, attempts were made to minimize damage to the tundra, but certain areas were needed for storage of construction materials. Today these areas, as well as the corridor along the pipeline itself, remain obvious scars, often dominated by unsuitable and long-dead grasses planted in misguided attempts at revegetation. Tundra plants cannot easily invade such mats of vegetation. Roads, even if only used once, also leave scars in the tundra (and in deserts). Post-glacial colonization can be studied to improve our understanding of what grows best in the cold peri-glacial habitats. The early introduction of nitrogen-fixing woody plants is often a crucial element to promote plant growth on glacial moraines. Restoration of human-caused analogs might include ripping or other surface treatments to alleviate compaction, followed by the introduction of nitrogen-fixing plants.

### 3.4.6   Links with other disturbances

Glaciers have links with many other disturbances, from volcanoes to rivers to human-induced climate change. In Iceland, the land of fire and ice, glaciers cover 10 percent of the country today and there are over 200 volcanoes. Occasionally, one erupts near or through glacial ice, causing massive flooding. These floodplains then become areas for farming, weed invasion, restoration and, inevitably, human misery when the cycle repeats itself and the farms and villages are destroyed. Glaciers reshape and destabilize the landscape creating conditions for secondary disturbances including floods, landslides, earthquakes, glacial rebound (uplift from release of the weight of the ice) and even volcanic activity. Even without humans, disturbance interactions form a complex mosaic often with subtle consequences for plants and animals. Adding humans greatly increases that complexity.

### 3.5   LESSONS FROM INFERTILE, UNSTABLE HABITATS

Infertile, unstable habitats are created by many natural phenomena. They form habitats that are nearly impossible to colonize and vegetation forms slowly at best. However, when volcanic surfaces, dunes and glacial forelands do stabilize, succession proceeds. The rooting force of plants dominates natural forces that reduce instability. Infertility is gradually ameliorated by inputs from other systems and by gradual weathering of the substrates. These habitats show that habitats created by humans that are infertile and unstable can be restored. Lessons learned by observing succession on these amazing landforms can be applied to habitats such as mine tailings.

BIBLIOGRAPHY

*Volcanoes*

Chester, D. (1993). *Volcanoes and Society*. London: Edward Arnold.
Dale, V.D., Swanson, F.J. and Crisafulli, C.M. (2005). *Ecological Responses to the 1980 Eruption of Mount St. Helens*. New York: Springer Science.
del Moral, R., Wood, D.M. and Titus, J.H. (2005). Proximity, microsites, and biotic interactions during early succession. In *Ecological Responses to the 1980 Eruption of Mount St. Helens*, ed. V.D. Dale, F.J. Swanson and C.M. Crisafulli. New York: Springer Science, pp. 93–110.

*Dunes*

Cloudsley-Thompson, J. (1977). *The Desert*. New York: G. P. Putnam's Sons.
Cowles, H. C. (1899). The ecological relations of the vegetation on the sand dunes of Lake Michigan. *Botanical Gazette*, **27**, 95–117.
Fagan, B. (2004). *The Long Summer: How Climate Change Changed Civilization*. New York: Basic Books.
Gelbspan, R. (1997). *The Heat is On*. New York: Addison–Wesley Publishing.
Postel, S. (1999). *Pillar of Sand: Can the Irrigation Miracle Last?* New York: W. W. Norton & Company.
Sears, P. B. (1980). *Deserts on the March*. Norman, OK: University of Oklahoma Press.
Walker, J., Thompson, C. H., Fergus, I. F. and Tunstall, B. R. (1981). Plant succession and soil development in coastal sand dunes of subtropical eastern Australia. In *Forest Succession: Concepts and Application*, ed. D. C. West, H. H. Shugart and D. B. Botkin. New York: Springer, pp. 107–31.

*Glaciers*

Chapin, F. S. III., Walker, L. R., Fastie, C. L. and Sharman, L. C. (1994). Mechanisms of primary succession following deglaciation at Glacier Bay, Alaska. *Ecological Monographs*, **64**, 149–75.
Matthews, J. A. (1992). *The Ecology of Recently Deglaciated Terrain: A Geoecological Approach to Glacier Forelands and Primary Succession*. Cambridge: Cambridge University Press.
Matthews, J. A. (1999). Disturbance regimes and ecosystem recovery on recently-deglaciated substrates. In *Ecosystems of Disturbed Ground, Ecosystems of the World 16*, ed. L. R. Walker. Amsterdam: Elsevier, pp. 17–37.
Sever, M. (2005). Melting glaciers reveal ancient bodies. *Geotimes*, **50**, 40–41.
Pearce, F. (2005). The flaw in the thaw. *New Scientist*, **187**, 27–30.
Pearce, F. (2005). Arctic ice shrinking as it feels the heat. *New Scientist*, **188**, 12.
Small, C. and Naumann, T. (2001). Holocene volcanism and the global distribution of human population. *Environmental Hazards*, **3**, 93–109.

# 4

# Infertile and stable habitats

## 4.1 STABLE HABITATS DEVELOP SLOWLY

Hard rock surfaces abound in nature, but they eventually develop a cover of vegetation. External forces soon begin to alter them by increasing their permeability to water and susceptibility to erosion. Even the slightest roughness or a small crack will allow plants to colonize such hard surfaces. Surface heterogeneity is caused by rapid temperature changes or by differential erosion of rock minerals. Most of these surfaces are created by lava (from Italian, *labes*, a falling, coined by Francesco Serao upon observing Vesuvius erupting in 1737), but steady erosion can also expose other types of rocks over time. Abrupt exposure of rock surfaces comes from sudden events such as landslides. Although hard surfaces are infertile, their stability allows slow-growing lichens to establish in dry habitats and mosses in wetter habitats. Cracks allow long-rooted woody plants, like trees, to gain a foothold. If successful, these large plants soon dominate exposed rocky surfaces, covering them with their dead leaves and accelerating the process of soil development and successional change in plant composition. On gentle terrain, succession may be slow, but it is inexorable. On steep slopes, gravity chronically removes nascent plant life, exposing new, abiotic surfaces. How plants cope with such stresses in natural habitats provides unique lessons for rehabilitation of analogous habitats caused by humans such as abandoned roads, parking lots and industrial rubble, quarries and walls. In this chapter, we will discuss two very different kinds of hard surfaces: lava and cliffs. How do plants manage to establish on these inhospitable surfaces?

---

**Box 4.1  A continuing drama**

Mt. Etna is the "Pearl of Sicily" and the largest volcano in Europe. It has erupted repeatedly in a history that spans over 3,500 years. Major eruptions were recorded in 475 BC, 396 BC (by Greek colonists), during the first century AD (Romans), in 866 (Saracens), 1136 (Normans), 1669 (Spanish), 1780, 1811, 1843 (all Bourbon and at least ten times since (Italians). Lava frequently oozes from new fissures and several destructive and lethal flows occurred between 2001 and 2005. A ski resort was destroyed at Rifugio Sapienza on the southern slope and the Mt. Etna Botanical Garden narrowly escaped. Yet the constant rain of tephra and episodic flows of lava have created rich agricultural land surrounding the volcano. Sicilians put great faith in protection by Santa Maria because many lava flows have stopped just short of villages — often at the steps of a church or chapel. They know the terrible potential of Mt. Etna to destroy, yet they have faith, despite contrary historical evidence, that future eruptions will not cause major harm. Mt. Etna is the lynchpin for tourism in eastern Sicily, to which Roger can attest. Hiking, climbing, guided tours and skiing continue to provide important economic stimulus. Lower slopes have been developed with many summer homes dotting the landscape, and quarries that mine lava for paving stones are common. Lemons, oranges, grapes and many other crops spread across the lower slopes.

---

## 4.2   LAVA

### 4.2.1  Introduction

There is an astounding legacy of legend and myth surrounding volcanoes. Where volcanoes erupt, people form myths and legends to explain and interpret the erratic behavior and the meaning of these ominous, looming presences for their lives. Mount Etna is central to Greek legends (e.g. Polyphemus the Cyclops) and literature from the Romans to the present day (Box 4.1). Volcanoes are central to stories about love entanglements, capricious deities, demons, deceptions and stories with environmental messages (Table 4.1).

Today, science is the usual way by which we seek to understand the natural world. The science of ecology owes much to the study of vegetation recovery on lava. Docters van Leeuven, DM, the Dutch director of the Java botanical garden, in 1930 visited the remnant of Krakatau (called Rakata), just as the new island called Anak Krakatau

Table 4.1. *Summary of myths about volcanoes.*

| Culture | Volcanoes and myth |
|---|---|
| Mexica, Mexico | Popocatépetl, Iztacchíhuat and Nevado de Toluca in a love triangle |
| Balinese, Bali | Agung the tallest mountain, and therefore the biggest deity. Probably stabilized the earthquake-ridden Bali, so it is considered the center of the world |
| Cowlitz and Klickitat people, Columbia basin | Loowit (Mount St. Helens), Pahtoe and Wyeast in a love triangle |
| Hawaiians, Hawaii | Pele sought refuge at Kilauea, whose muse, Aila'au, then disappeared. Today, Hawaiians honor and propitiate her with food and flowers |
| Icelandic tradition | In AD 1000, theological debate raged at Thingvellir, where Europe meets America. Lava spewed forth and Christians won the argument because the calamity happened on the Pagan watch |
| Shinto, Honshu | Fuji-san is the home of many venerated spirits (*kami*) |
| Javanese, Java | Tengger Crater formed by an ogre seeking the hand of a princess and deceived by a king |
| Klamath people, California | Mt. Mazama (Llao) and Mt. Shasta (Skell) fought battles analogous to Christian battles between angels and demons |
| Maori, New Zealand | Tongariro, Taranaki and Ruapehu in a love triangle |
| Canary Islands | Spain's tallest mountain, Mt. Teide, is sacred to the indigenous people, the Guanches, although it is believed to house demons |
| Philippines | Mt. Mayon, the remains of the jealous uncle Magayon, formed in retribution for trying to keep his niece and a warrior apart |

was emerging from the sunken caldera in the Sunda Straight between Java and Sumatra (Indonesia). Well aware that his was the first serious scientific study of recovery, his 500 page monograph was comprehensive. More importantly, his many ecological observations and predictions about succession proved to be true. Notably, he thought that trajectories would not lead to a return of the types of forests noted before the eruption because of dispersal limitations. Hideo Tagawa, the eminent Japanese ethnobotanist and ecologist, lives in the shadow of the unremittingly active volcano Sakurajima. His work on lavas of different ages has resulted in better understanding of establishment processes and dispersal mechanisms. He too studied Krakatau, helping to build an understanding of assembly processes. William A. Eggler, an American ecologist, began work on ancient lavas in Idaho, where he emphasized the importance of safe-sites. However, his best-known work was the early characterization of colonization on Parícutin, a volcano that erupted in 1946 in a Mexican cornfield. In his Hawaiian studies, Eggler later introduced quantitative methods to the study of lava. All of these seminal studies were crucial to the advancement of succession theory and facilitated detailed modern studies of ecosystem assembly.

Studies of lava provide many lessons for the restoration of human and natural landscapes. We are learning how to reclaim habitats that are rocky, with little water or fertility. Lava surfaces have been studied intensively since the early twentieth century, but remain a huge challenge for those wishing to restore them.

### 4.2.2   Physical setting

Many volcanoes are on the edges of continents. They result when tectonic plates collide. Thus, they occur on the "Ring of Fire", which extends from Antarctica up the west coast of the Americas, around Alaska, down the Kamchatka Peninsula, throughout the Kuril Islands and Japan, to the Philippines and Indonesia and on to New Zealand. In other sites, the plates are moving apart, leading to rift volcanoes. The Mid-Atlantic Ridge supports rift volcanoes in the Canary Islands and Iceland, while the African Rift Valley hosts several huge, active volcanoes such as Mount Nyiragongo (Rwanda). The third category includes volcanic systems formed over hotspots. Most notable are the Hawaiian Islands in the central Pacific Ocean and Réunion in the Indian Ocean, but Yellowstone Valley (Wyoming, USA) is also a huge volcano supported by a hotspot that is considered active. Shield volcanoes are built up by large quantities of lava that ooze from many vents over long periods. Flows are hot and fluid, and so are often very long. Flows from Mount Etna (Sicily) reached Catania, 30 km to the south, in 1663. This sequence of flows partially covered a city that had suffered seven such burials since the original Greek town was founded in the eighth century BC. Flows from Mauna Loa, the largest shield volcano on Earth, have created much of the Island of Hawaii. Shield volcanoes are generally massive, with relatively gentle slopes. They are formed primarily of lava, but they also produce tephra and pyroclastic flows.

---

**Box 4.2  A distant roar**

Every three weeks, almost to the hour, a distant roar could be heard
from Lawrence's house in the town of Volcano on the island of
Hawaii. However, it wasn't from the main dormant crater of Kilauea
Iki just 30 m from his door. That crater greeted tourists, including
Mark Twain, with bubbling lava between 1823 and 1924 but its dull
black surface is now crossed with trails. Smelly sulfur vents still
suggest some activity below ground. The roaring sound came
instead from a distant vent of the same volcano called Pu'u O'o, the
mysterious one (see Fig. 4.6). By traveling 3 km downhill, Lawrence
could watch the distant glow as tephra and lava spewed from
this newest addition. Between July 1986 and June 1989 he saw a
lush rainforest transformed into a 250 m tall cinder cone.
What awesome, unstoppable power!

---

Stratovolcanoes, more common than shield volcanoes, are sometimes called composite volcanoes. They produce lava, but also copious
amounts of tephra. Because they are usually on tectonic boundaries,
they are also associated with large earthquakes. Familiar examples of
these volcanoes include Mt. Rainier (USA), Mt. Mayon (Philippines) and
Mt. Fuji (Japan). Lava can be exuded from a volcano in one of two basic
ways. During explosive eruptions, lava that is high in silica (called
rhyolite) blasts into the air. Low silica lava (basalt) oozes in what are
called effusive eruptions and can flow for many kilometers but lava
flows are less dangerous than explosive eruptions (Box 4.2). Lava can
emerge as *a'a* (Hawaiian for rough, stony lava, or to burn). It is crinkly
and full of cracks. If lava flows smoothly due to high viscosity, it is
*pahoehoe* (Hawaiian for smooth, unbroken lava). Pahoehoe lava is often
hummocky or ropy on the surface. Pillow basalt is formed when lava
flows into water. A solid crust forms immediately, but it continues
to ooze.

When lava cools in stressful habitats, lichens commonly dominate
early primary succession. In Alaska, the bitter cold limits seed plants,
while on Mt. Etna the summer drought does the same. When the lava
fractures, the pace of succession increases. Lava flows that also receive
tephra can develop more rapidly, as has occurred on Sakurajima (Japan)
and on Mt. Tolbachik (Kamchatka, Russia; Fig. 4.1). Cracks permit the
establishment of ferns, shrubs and trees and tephra mulches the
surface. On Tolbachik, at high elevation and latitude, cracks in the *a'a*
lava supported herbs such as fireweed and ryegrass, while lichens and

Fig. 4.1  Mt. Tolbachik (Kamchatka, Russian) is a young, active volcano. Viscous lava can take strange forms; though 400 years old, severe climate and impervious surfaces slow the rate of succession.

Fig. 4.2  Pahoehoe lava (Kilauea, Hawaii) is difficult to invade on the dry side of this island. It typically lacks vegetation for many decades.

mosses dominated the exposed surfaces. Woody species remained rare during the first 50 years. Succession on pahoehoe lava (Fig. 4.2; Fig. 4.3), which lacks establishment sites, is usually slower, though may be accelerated if there are cracks and ample moisture. Some surfaces

Fig. 4.3 Pahoehoe lava can support vegetation in cracks. Here, ferns find a suitable environment.

estimated to be over 1,000 years old are still dominated by lichens. Succession in Kamchatka is five to ten times slower than in southern Japan, even though the lavas are similar, due to the cooler growing season temperatures in Kamchatka. These comparisons demonstrate how growing conditions and substrates affect succession rates.

### 4.2.3   Lava in the lives of humans

*Lava in the human psyche*

Volcanoes capture our imaginations and instill awe and fear. Myths serve many important functions in human cultures and volcanoes are often deified, but we continue to underestimate their episodic power. Maoris, Icelanders, North American Indians and many others have myths to explain their volatile activity (Table 4.1). The stories related below describe a variety of volcanic surfaces, including lava and pyroclastic flows. Each attempts to explain the observed landscape within a particular cultural paradigm.

Volcanoes often occur in groups, leading to startlingly similar legends in disparate parts of the world. Love triangles are a major theme. Loowit, now called Mount St. Helens, and her consorts Pahtoe (Mt. Adams) and Wyeast (Mt. Hood) caused great mischief in the Pacific Northwest (USA), resulting in the Columbia River Gorge and three restless volcanoes. A classic myth told among the Tenochca tribe of the Mexica, a Nahua-speaking people that dominated the Valley of Mexico when encountered by Cortés, concerns Popocatépetl. He was a warrior married to the lovely Iztacchíhuat, who also was the object of desire of Nevado de Toluca. The vigorous battles fought between these mythic warriors created the continental divide and the trans-Mexico volcanic range that lies between the continents. Eventually, Popo flung a chunk of ice and knocked the head from the Nevado de Toluca. This is why Nevado is flat-topped. The legend fits the geological events as inferred by volcanologists.

Another particularly tragic love triangle involved the Maori heroes Taranaki and Ruapehu. Each loved the beautiful maiden Tongariro (Mt. Ngauruhoe). When Tongariro could not decide between the two warriors, a violent clash of these titans restructured much of the New Zealand landscape. Taranaki tried to crush Ruapehu with rocks, ultimately ruining his cone; Ruapehu retaliated by spraying scalding water across the land. Under a hail of ejecta, Taranaki retreated to the sea where he now broods, sure to seek revenge. To this day, some Maoris refuse to live between Taranaki and Ruapehu. Taranaki has had eight small explosive eruptions since about 7K BP. A major eruption occurred in 1755, suggesting that Taranaki remains angry.

Mt. Etna, Greek for "I burn," was known to Plato and later to Aeschylus as the mouth of Hades. It was home to Hephaestus, the Greek god of fire and metallurgy and to Typhon, a 100-headed monster and rebellious son of Gaia. Zeus exiled Typhon to beneath Etna, explaining the many eruptions that have occurred since. Homer placed Polyphemus, the chief of the Cyclops clan, who almost ate Odysseus, in nearby caves. Virgil, later to be drafted as Dante's guide in the Inferno, wrote in BC 29:

> How often have we seen Etna, her furnace-walls asunder riven,
> In billowy floods boil o'er the Cyclops' fields,
> And roll down globes of fire and molten rocks.

The Roman god of fire, Vulcan, was believed to inhabit the small, rather unimpressive Aeolian Island now known by the eponymous name Vulcano (Plate 6). This is why we call fire mountains volcanoes, rather than *etnas*, as they were known to the Greeks. Dante Alighieri (early fourteenth century) described Etna (*Mongibello*) in the *Inferno* as Vulcan's forge.

Modern Europeans loved Etna and it became part of the Grand Tour. Goethe climbed its pristine slopes in 1787, and marveled at the

> **Box 4.3 Traditional knowledge is often right!**
>
> On Sakurajima, the large, continuously active volcano in the harbor of the Japanese city Kagoshima, a schoolyard is perched on the lava from the massive 1914 eruption. At that time of great global unrest, Sakurajima threatened another cataclysm. Yet geologists, teachers and the learned professionals urged the population to be calm . . . nothing bad would happen. The Shinto priests, in contrast, urged the people to flee. Great loss of life was thus averted when the cataclysm did occur. When Roger visited this school, he found a plaque attached to a large lava boulder that commemorates the wisdom of the peasants. Roughly translated, it says "*Put not your faith in science.*" Here we counsel prudence and common sense, and a measured attention to the advice of science made more modest by past miscalculations.

view of the Sicilian coast. In 1799, after Admiral Horatio Nelson had won the battle of the Nile, Ferdinand IV made him the Duke of Bronte (Greek for Cyclops) and granted him an estate on the western slope of Etna. Since then the English, in particular, have been drawn to the nearby ancient town of Taormina.

Myths about volcanoes abound in Japanese folk tales. The perfect cone of Mt. Fuji is sacred in both the Shinto and Buddhist beliefs, and is a major "mecca" for pilgrims and tourists alike. Fuji is central to the creed of Shinto, which is a veneration of nature, including animate and inanimate objects. *Kami*, loosely interpreted as spirits that can influence human destiny, reside in such places, and may respond to prayer. Buddhists see climbing as a metaphor for spiritual enlightenment, and because Fuji is the tallest Japanese volcano, it is an important site. *Fuji* has many meanings in Japanese (e.g. strong, mighty), and may come from "spirit of fire" in the indigenous Ainu. The immediate area is not densely populated and the mountain is thoroughly instrumented, so that it is likely that sufficient warnings of an eruption will be available to avert large loss of life. To the south, the nearly urban volcano Sakurajima vents continuously (Box 4.3).

In Java (Indonesia), people believe that an ogre using a coconut shell carved the Tengger Crater. To win the hand of the King's beautiful daughter, he had to complete this Herculean task in a day. As he neared completion, the King got his servants to cause a ruckus, waking the cocks, who signaled daybreak. In disgust, the ogre tossed the coconut aside and it became a small crater. The trench became a sea, and the ogre died ... of grief or exhaustion, who can say? Thus, the landscape is explained by the actions of these mythic beings.

Nearby, the Philippines have many legends associated with volcanoes. Mt. Mayon is central to the story of another beautiful princess. Her jealous uncle Magayon was so possessive that no one dared to court the princess. One day, a brave, possibly stupid warrior convinced her to elope. With Magayon close behind, they prayed for salvation, which was delivered in the form of a lahar that swept down to bury him. Today, many believe that Mount Mayon's constant eruptions are Magayon, frothing at the indignity. The facts fit the story.

### Economic values of lava

Today, many volcanoes support ecotourism as well as large local populations on their slopes, so risks to humans from volcanic eruptions are growing. Guided tours bring thousands of people annually to glowing flows on the slopes of Mt. Etna and to the steaming south shore of the island of Hawaii. Other popular volcanoes are Mt. Kilimanjaro in east Africa, Ruapehu in New Zealand, Mt. Tolbachik on the Kamchatka Peninsula, Mt. Hekla in Iceland and many volcanoes in Japan, Alaska and the northwestern USA. Volcanoes attract most tourists when they are in eruptive phases, exactly when the danger is greatest.

Lava itself has economic value. Dense black lava is mined from several quarries on Mt. Etna and used for paving roads. Etnaean lava is also used to make beautiful counter tops and stone-inlay furniture. A special form of lava, called alvar, is used in Peru for building stunning churches. When silica-rich lava enters water, obsidian is often formed. Obsidian is common in Iceland and on the Sicilian island of Lipari, and is scattered throughout the world. It is valued for its ornamental attraction, but once obsidian was the essential ingredient in cutting tools and weapons. Volcanoes also provide a grey–green mineral called olivine and sulfur, a key ingredient in fertilizers.

### Human tragedies continue

Lava covers much of the earth, but very large and destructive flows are uncommon. Villages on Hawaii and a ski resort on Mt. Etna are among recent victims. Though dwarfed in magnitude by other recent natural disasters, lava eruptions can turn deadly. The steep stratovolcano Nyiragongo in the African Rift Valley in the Republic of the Congo is only about 19 km north of Goma. It periodically contains the world's largest lava lake. In 1977, the crater walls fractured and the lake drained, flowing rapidly downslope, destroying several villages and a large, but undetermined, number of people. The region remains heavily populated. The lava lake re-formed so that in 2002 it contributed to flows from a new fissure that broke open along 18 km of the mountain. The town of Goma was devastated by one flow in 2002, which killed 45 people and destroyed 15 percent of the town. This was the most destructive lava flow in the last 400 years. Generally, lava flows cause few deaths, but great destruction. People can move faster than most lava flows.

### 4.2.4   Ecological responses to lava flows

Lava provides one of the most dramatic settings for the study of colonizing virgin land. Natural recolonization of lavas demonstrates many general principles of succession. The rate of succession is altered by factors including type of lava, climate, local environmental stress, fertility, dispersal factors and biotic interactions. Here we focus on factors affecting establishment under harsh conditions.

*Establishment*

The surface characteristics of lava are the major determinants of plant success. On the dry slopes of Mt. Etna, lavas from 1886 have only a few scattered vascular plants, though some of these are shrubs. Younger lavas have only mosses and lichens (Fig. 4.4). On Mauna Loa, Hawaii, flows of similar age develop at different rates depending on their surfaces. In the same area, rainforest developed within 100 years on the rainy windward slopes while lichens dominated the dry side. What permits the establishment of that first seed plant? Seeds are trapped by cracks caused by frost (Fig. 4.5). If enough organic material has accumulated in the crack and drought does not kill the seedling, it may survive in the safe-site. In contrast to lahars or pyroclastic flows, it takes many years for plants to establish on lava.

*Development*

The first colonists will alter the immediate environment, so succession accelerates in their immediate vicinity. For example, on Mt. Etna, two flows from the late nineteenth century that are only a few hundred

Fig. 4.4  Lava on Mt. Etna (Sicily, Italy) is covered primarily by lichens and mosses for decades. Vascular plants are confined to the cracks between lava blocks on this surface after 125 years.

Fig. 4.5  Young pahoehoe lava formed in 1990. The contact with existing forest near the buried town of Kalapana (Hawaii) shows how after only 15 years plants have found the cracks and are beginning to reclaim this lava.

Fig. 4.6 A kipuka (area of surviving vegetation) on the Big Island of Hawaii. Note tree ferns and *Metrosideros* trees near a new cinder cone called Pu'u O'o.

meters apart differed in the presence of nitrogen-fixing shrubs. Where brooms (*Spartium*, *Genista*) occurred, species richness was several times and cover three times greater than in their absence. This facilitation probably resulted from a combination of factors, including shade, enhanced capture of seeds, wind-driven organic matter and *in situ* nitrogen fixation. On older sites, competition began to occur as the shrubs created dense shade, thus shifting the species composition beneath the canopy compared to the more open surroundings without shrubs. Over the centuries on these dry lavas, shrubs attract birds and facilitate dispersal. After many centuries, oaks finally establish.

### Patterns

During early development, lava demonstrates several patterns that result from landscape effects. *Dagale* (Italian) and *kipukas* (Hawaiian; Fig. 4.6) are types of intact island that have escaped the lava and may contribute to rapid colonization (like nunataks escaping glaciation). They are legacies that can provide an immediate source of colonists and allow succession to be "jump started." Invading species also can establish in the legacies, and then fan out. Wind direction alters the rate of development, so that flows of equal age show distinct patterns of species composition with distances from lava edges that depend on local prevailing winds.

### 4.2.5   Human responses to lava

More people are at risk from volcanoes today than ever before. In 2005, the Mount Manaro volcano began eruptions that threaten thousands on a small island in Vanuatu (New Hebrides). This island is symbolic of the millions of people who literally live "under the volcano". Lava is the slowest form of dangerous volcanism, but it is inexorable. Throughout the world, humans have learned to cope with lava flows, including relocating to new areas when necessary. During the recent and continuing eruptions of Kilauea, enterprising Hawaiians have set up stands to sell crafts. For one dollar, you can buy a coconut to plant in the new lava (in a crack, to be sure). Thus, enterprise is accelerating succession on this lava, perhaps forming a novel trajectory.

The 1973 eruption on Heimaey, an important island off the Icelandic coast, destroyed much of the only fishing village on the island. However, in the largest effort on record to stop lava, the villagers sprayed seawater on the lava and managed to stop it before the harbor became sealed. The ubiquitous occurrence of lava flows on Sicily also requires an aggressive approach to reclamation. Lava is quickly reclaimed and roads rebuilt soon after it has cooled.

Lava provides a model for the restoration of relatively impervious surfaces such as pavements, landfills, mine tailings and rubble heaps. Pavements and hard-packed gravel occur in parking lots, old railroad beds, abandoned airports and abandoned roads (Fig. 4.7). Old roads, for example, can be fractured by drilling holes to improve porosity and capture seeds, thus speeding the creation of safe-sites. On steeper sites, physical stabilization using local materials will permit plants to establish. A heterogeneous surface, combined with sowing of relevant species and improving fertility, will greatly hasten the obliteration of roads and the resumption of biologically productive communities. Restoration of impervious surfaces is considered successful if there is complex growth–form structure, even if species diversity remains low.

### 4.2.6   Links with other forms of disturbance

Lava is most closely linked to the other forms of volcanism. Lava eruptions can occur with or without explosive tephra eruptions. Because tephra is more readily colonized than lava, it may hasten the

Fig. 4.7 Plants begin to colonize cracks between two reflectors on an abandoned road in Lake Mead National Recreation Area (Nevada, USA). Such cracks are the first requirement for succession because they offer a refuge in which seeds can germinate and establish (compare with Fig. 4.3).

recolonization of lava. The 400 year-old lava on Mount Tolbachik (Kamchatka Peninsula) was scarcely colonized until tephra coated it in 1978, which permitted the establishment of wind-dispersed woody species.

Lava is also linked to glaciers. Though beyond our notice, volcanoes commonly erupt through glaciers in Antarctica. Mount Erebus, nearly 3,800 m tall at latitude 77°S, is a large, active volcano of the Strombolian type that ejects bombs through a lake of molten lava. Being on a rift zone, Antarctic volcanoes are strangely similar to their Icelandic counterparts. Both are simmering mountains, clothed in ice. When they do erupt, masses of lava pour onto the ice. Lava blocks melt ice to form temporary lakes. When the lava dam bursts, the lakes are liberated to cause massive inundations. An interesting feature of hot lava meeting cold ice is the formation of flat-topped mountains called *tuyas*, an Inuit word. They occur in Iceland where volcanoes grow under ice, then emerge on top of the ice and spread like mushroom caps whose edges fall off when the ice melts, leaving a flat-topped cone (Fig. 4.8).

Fig. 4.8 Tuyas are common in Iceland. This landscape of lava and glaciers is often punctuated by steep-sided tuyas formed when lava from a volcano emerges from underneath a glacier.

Lava has also created extensive landscapes such as the Columbia Basin of Washington and the Deccan Traps in India. These massive, ancient basaltic lava floods formed tablelands and steep cliffs where rivers (such as the Columbia) cut down, forming impressive canyons. These cliffs bear similarities to the steep rock outcrops discussed in the next section.

## 4.3    CLIFFS

### 4.3.1    Introduction

Cliffs, or vertical rock surfaces, are a dramatic part of almost every landscape on earth. Cliffs dominate some landscapes, including karst regions in China and Vietnam, sandstone canyons in Utah, USA and shorelines throughout the world. Even the relatively flat plains of central Canada or Siberia have outcrops with vertical surfaces along river drainages or where there is erosion-resistant rock. Cliffs are hard to plow, harder to log, harder still to build roads through and nearly impossible to build on. The result is that cliffs are often the last refuges of rare plants, virgin forests and protected ecosystems. Many plants are also restricted to the unique habitats that cliffs offer. Vertical surfaces also attract humans – for food, shelter, defense, mining, sport and

Fig. 4.9  Cliff dwellings in Mesa Verde National Park (Colorado, USA).
The ancient ones (Anasazi), ancestors of the Hopi people, lived in such
protected cliff homes until adverse climate changes forced them away.

many other reasons. Caves formed by overhanging cliffs at Lamington
National Park (Queensland, Australia) provided shelter for Aboriginal
people for thousands of years. For hundreds of years, cliffs provided safe
homes for natives of the southwestern USA (Fig. 4.9). In this section,
we will explore the geology, biology and human fascination with cliffs
and examine attempts to restore vertical surfaces that are both natural
and man-made.

Rocky surfaces are nearly as infertile as lava surfaces and are
surprisingly stable, once the forces that caused them have ceased.
Tectonic forces such as uplift along fault lines, erosion from wind
and water and humans carving rocks from mines and quarries all
produce rocky surfaces. They can have nearly vertical surfaces, such
as the 1,000 m tall sandstone cliffs of Zion National Park in southern
Utah (USA) and the bluffs along the Great Ocean Road of western
Victoria (Australia), or they may be inclined talus slopes. They may

even be flat, like the granite domes of the Sierra Nevada, California (USA), the calcareous alvars of Wisconsin (USA), Estonia and Italy or the sandstone *tepuis* of Amazonia. Our emphasis is on the nearly vertical surfaces, especially cliff faces and their associated talus slopes. Understanding the dynamics of vegetation on cliffs provides insight into how to better manage rocky surfaces for stability and enhanced biodiversity.

### 4.3.2   Physical setting

Along most geological fault zones, such as where tectonic plates collide, uplift can create cliffs. Cliffs can also form from differential erosion of existing rock layers. Physical and chemical weathering then occur, making the exposed rock surfaces subject to erosion. Freeze–thaw processes can rapidly break up many rock types. Carbonate rocks also are susceptible to active dissolution by water. Steep-sided karst hills in Puerto Rico, for example, appear to lean downwind because rain driven by the northeast trade winds dissolves the windward edge and calcium precipitates on the leeward side. Erosion by water, wind and gravity remove weathered particles from cliffs.

Erosion depends on the hardness of the rock and the variability in hardness within and across rock types. Sometimes the surrounding rock may erode, leaving vertical surfaces of erosion-resistant rock, such as old lava plugs in the crater floors of ancient volcanoes in Hawaii and remnant basaltic plugs from recent volcanoes. Where soft, erosive rocks underlie harder rocks, pronounced cliff faces (Plate 7) or even overhangs occur. Depending on the rock type, such undercutting sometimes occurs when massive blocks of stone erode away. Gravity removes loosened rocks from a cliff by causing undercut rocks to fall, by toppling rocks that are jointed both vertically and horizontally or by rotational slides or slumps. More gradual cliff faces or even gentle slopes result from erosion of layers of soft rocks. Variable hardness within a rock surface can lead to variable erosion and to a rough, pockmarked surface. Therefore, the steepest cliffs with the smoothest surfaces are from homogeneous, hard rocks such as lava (Fig. 4.10).

Cliffs are eroded by water along seashores or riverbeds and by steady wind in arid regions. Coastal cliffs are ubiquitous and result from changing sea levels and wave erosion. Many different features result, depending again on rock hardness and heterogeneity. Offshore resistant rocks called stacks delight coastal visitors and nesting birds (Fig. 4.11). Caves and arches can form and provide both unique habitats for fish and

Fig. 4.10 Dyrholaey Beach (Iceland) with columnar basalt. Lava cooling under intense pressure often breaks up into such columnar joints.

Fig. 4.11 Haystacks are common on the Great Ocean Road (Victoria, Australia). Such isolated islets are prime nesting grounds for sea birds.

bats but also such dramatic tourist attractions as blowholes. River erosion sometimes creates dramatic cliffs such as those along the Grand Canyon (USA) that result from centuries of erosion through layers of rocks with varying resistance. Waterfalls often form where rivers meet resistant surface rocks underlain by softer rocks. Wind sculpts cliffs in arid areas, particularly where sandstones dominate and windblown sand scours cliff surfaces to cause intricate and smooth-edged pockets and arches.

A cliff begins abruptly where a more or less flat surface meets a nearly vertical face (Fig. 4.12). The cliff face is often interrupted with a variety of ledges, cracks, caves and overhangs, each providing microsites for the accumulation of moisture, nutrients and organic matter and for plant colonization and animal nests. A talus slope frequently forms at the base of a cliff where rocks tumble down and accumulate. If erosion on the cliff face is active, the talus remains barren. The upper platforms or ramps of some cliffs can be pockmarked with scars or sockets – the source of boulders found below. These scars and sockets are often indicated by the lack of a weathered patina or lichen cover, indicating recent boulder removal.

### 4.3.3   Cliffs in the lives of humans

Human history began in the Great Rift zone in northeastern Africa, where huge cliffs bound fertile plains to the east and west. These cliffs and associated caves were essential to human evolution. Ever since, cliffs have both served and fascinated humans in many practical and less tangible ways. Historically, humans used cliffs for shelter, food collection, hunting and refuge. They also had spiritual, artistic and political purposes. Today we still enjoy the aesthetics of cliffs themselves and the views from them as well as the recreation possibilities they provide.

Early humans found dry, comfortable and easily defended dwellings in caves eroded from cliff bases (Neanderthals in Europe) or up on the actual cliffs (Anasazi in southwestern USA). Some early humans built homes on tops of cliffs or mesas (Incas at Machu Pichu, Peru). Cliffs were also a source of food. Hunters certainly used cliffs as lookouts or places for signaling each other. Birds' eggs and herbs could be collected with relative ease because there were many paths and crannies arrayed on the cliff face. Large game could be herded over cliffs to their death or cliffs could provide backdrops for corralling animals into narrow

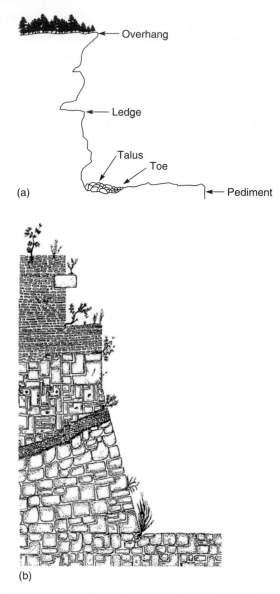

(a)

(b)

Fig. 4.12 Typical cliffs with (a) physical features and (b) microsites for plants and nesting birds. Modified from Larson *et al.* (2000). Reprinted with the permission of Cambridge University Press.

Fig. 4.13  Thingvellier (Iceland) was the seat of Iceland's first democratic assembly, the Althing, from AD 930 to the nineteenth century. Iceland sits on the Mid-Atlantic ridge. At Thingvellir, a river meanders along the fault line, while shear basaltic cliffs form a natural amphitheater from which the rules were shouted for all to hear and know.

locations where they could be stoned or speared. Some cliffs provided readily accessible rocks such as obsidian and flint for tools.

Less practical uses of cliffs have also long been a part of human culture. Rock art, often thousands of years old, has survived around the world, giving us glimpses of past cultures. Often the purpose of the art is not known. Was it adolescent graffiti? Spiritual musings? Signposts to good hunting areas? More overtly spiritual uses of cliffs include the two Bamiyan Buddha statues (53 and 36 m tall) that were carved out of a cliff in Afghanistan in the third century AD. Unfortunately, Taliban forces demolished these masterworks in 2001. The political use of cliffs started in AD 930 when Icelanders chose a dramatic set of cliffs at Thingvellir on the Mid-Atlantic Ridge for their parliament, the Althing (Fig. 4.13). The cliffs, one in Europe, the other in America, provided speakers with a bully pulpit and voice amplification, while the river dividing the adjacent cliffs provided a handy place to drown those guilty of severe crimes.

Modern uses of cliffs continue to be both practical and intangible. Dams are ideally built where riverbanks form cliffs (Hoover Dam, USA). Icelanders currently use huge nets to scoop puffins from the sky as they approach their cliff-top nests high above the sea. Miners and geologists explore rock outcrops for signs of ore and botanists collect the slow-growing plants as bonsai specimens. Unfortunately, cliffs also provide an easy way to dispose of garbage, used cars or even corpses, especially when a community, road or trail abuts the top of the cliff. Such behavior impacts rock climbers and other outdoor enthusiasts while damaging vistas and cliff vegetation and promoting undesirable scavengers. Clifftops are now considered prime real estate for homes with a view, especially along urbanized coastlines. Recreational uses of cliffs include hang gliding, base-jumping and ice and rock climbing. Intangible uses of cliffs include their scenic value to tourists, especially when they have cascading waterfalls. Such popular attractions include Niagara Falls (USA), Gullfoss (Iceland) and Iguaçu Falls along the Brazil–Argentina border. Switzerland and other mountainous countries capitalize on cliffs to increase the scenic enjoyment of trams, cog railways and ski lifts. Cliffs have often been featured in artwork from many countries, particularly in Asia. They are embedded in our human psyche as symbols of excitement, danger, untamed scenery and contemplation. Movies and even our vocabulary reflect this fascination (e.g. "cliff-hanger"). Advertisements featuring vehicles or computer users perched on cliff edges, free of all typical restraints, also capitalize on our emotional responses to cliffs.

Cliffs also pose challenges to humans. Collapses of cliffs or unstable talus slopes have damaged residences and regularly close roads in many mountainous regions. For example, late in 2005 the interstate highway east of Seattle (USA) was blocked for several days after a cliff collapsed, killing three people as they drove innocently by. Humans have also created cliffs during open pit mining for coal, quarrying for granite or marble and the construction of roads, tunnels and buildings. Cliffs are therefore well integrated into human lives.

### 4.3.4  Ecology of cliffs

Plants colonize cliff surfaces only where the surface allows soils to develop, typically in horizontal cracks or ledges. Colonization of vertical cracks and exposed rock surfaces can take centuries, even in favorable climates, due to the lack of soil accumulation. Moss can develop on moist vertical surfaces, such as on walls in humid climates. The parliament building in Reykjavik, Iceland has a wall covered with dense moss mats. The architect originally worried that this moss was not

---

**Box 4.4  Precarious habitat for a species on the brink**

Perched on a small ledge, Lawrence reaches high over his head
to slip the thermometer into the tiny pocket of soil beneath
the lovely white saxifrage. Growing only on three cliffs in central
Vermont, this rare plant has survived since the glaciers melted
back twelve thousand years ago. Despite moist seeps running
down the cliff and warm temperatures, a lack of soil
development has stopped the lush forests from gaining
a foothold on these cliffs.

---

developing fast enough. Then someone suggested fastening newspaper
to the wall. This provided just enough surface texture for the moss to
grow and today the wall is covered with a wonderfully lush growth of
moss that insulates the building and thus conserves energy.

Plant growth on cliffs is very limited due to the combined effects
of minimal soil and occasional severe erosion. Large plants are rare as
they collapse from their own weight. Trees with long roots typically
colonize cracks while grasses with shallow but fibrous roots and
perennial herbs are often found on small ledges. Soil fertility can be
high where birds roost or nest, but it is normally quite low because there
is little soil to retain either atmospheric or waterborne inputs.
Temperature extremes (hot during full sun exposure, cold during the
night with no insulating vegetation layer) can also reduce development
by retarding decomposition and killing plants. Drought limits plant
growth on most cliffs because of a lack of direct precipitation, lack of
soil to absorb moisture and high evaporation rates. The cliff flora is
therefore often distinct from the surrounding vegetation. For example,
cliffs in central Vermont (USA) have small saxifrages typically found
only in arctic tundra hundreds of kilometers further north (Box 4.4).
Cliff flora is generally dominated by hardy perennials that grow very
slowly, such as eastern white cedars on the Niagara Escarpment in
Ontario (Canada), junipers in Swedish Lapland or the rare Wollemi pine,
recently discovered on cliffs in New South Wales (Australia). Despite
these difficult growing conditions, cliff vegetation can represent a large
fraction of the diversity of plant species in a region. Causal factors for
this diversity probably include isolation from human-related disturbances such as fire and grazing.

Species composition does not change very rapidly on most cliffs.
Succession can occur when new cliff faces (such as quarry walls) are
exposed, but most cliff vegetation is somewhat stable, once all niches

are filled. Annual species that depend on establishing from seed each year are rare, presumably because there is so little turnover in regeneration sites. Success on a cliff is achieved by literally hanging on, growing slowly and not investing too much in reproduction.

Animals typically associated with cliffs include birds, particularly raptors and sea birds. Cliffs provide protection from predation and aid raptors in hunting. Coastal cliffs provide easy access to fishing for sea birds, which are not always the strongest fliers. The young of some seabirds, such as thick-billed murres, jump directly into the ocean before they can fly. Dense colonies of sea birds, limited only by nesting space, apparently deter predators. Puffins can reach densities of more than 1,000 burrows per hectare on cliffs in Iceland (Plate 8) and northern Great Britain, and the little penguin forms dense colonies in the sandy cliffs of southern Victoria (Australia).

Many other animals use cliffs for feeding, reproduction and escape from predators. Wild goats and sheep of various kinds move with amazing agility up near-vertical surfaces. Rodents enjoy rock crevices, bats use caves and snakes and lizards benefit from the warm sun on bare rocks. Beetles, mites and spiders are also very common, sometimes associated with mammalian nests. In fact, animals common to city landscapes, like pigeons, may have originally inhabited cliffs. And humans often seek cliffs for the view and the thrill of the edge (Fig. 4.14).

### 4.3.5   Human responses

Humans may be more likely to create a cliff than rehabilitate one. However, when humans create vertical surfaces such as road embankments or quarries, there is sometimes considerable effort made to stabilize or revegetate them. Humans inevitably make roads and railways across mountain slopes, and then periodically widen them to improve traffic flow. Any cut in a slope destabilizes it, and erosion follows. Generally, the problem is soil creep, but sudden rock falls can close roads, crush vehicles and block rivers. Revegetation of cliffs might stop soil erosion, but when the slope is undercut enough to allow rock falls, more contouring is usually done, reducing the steepness of the slope. In the worst cases, the road can be built into the slope (e.g. Swiss trains), out away from the slope on pylons (as in Arthur's Pass, New Zealand) or abandoned altogether.

Urban embankments, quarry walls and other highly visible man-made surfaces receive much attention. Embankments, such as

Fig. 4.14  Stunning scenery in Canyon Lands National Park (Utah, USA) attracts tourists from around the world. (Courtesy of Simon Baker.)

found around highway interchanges, are often stabilized with concrete walls or rock fill, but sometimes they are planted with grasses or other ground cover. Road embankments in southern California, USA and elsewhere are covered by ice plant (a native of South Africa), a low-growing and colorful ground cover that tolerates salt spray (it also grows on coastal dunes) and sulfur fumes (it grows on an active volcano in New Zealand). The polluted air along highways in California has some of these same characteristics. Sound barriers along highways are ugly until they are covered by vines and masked by trees. Studies of cliffs have provided information on how to grow plants on barriers, and newly constructed ones now present rough surfaces and articulations to facilitate plant growth. Quarries can become good laboratories for how to revegetate damaged natural cliff faces. However, revegetation of cliffs is complicated because most are habitat islands. Therefore, few likely colonists are available and most are not particularly adapted to long-distance dispersal. Thus, what colonizes cliffs provides insights into colonization of habitat islands in general. Determining which species survive direct planting or sowing onto a cliff helps us understand the nature of safe-sites for plant establishment and growth.

### 4.3.6   Links with other disturbances

Many other disturbances can create vertical surfaces, so the study of cliffs integrates the biological responses to vertical features found on many landforms, regardless of origin. Tephra and lava tend to produce level terrain except when passing over existing slopes or landing on the central volcanic cone. Glaciers carve the landscape, often leaving cliffs of harder rock. Even compacted dunes are easily eroded to form steep surfaces and water and wind sculpt cliffs from sandstone. One need only visit the canyons of the American southwest or the Great Ocean Road along the coast of Victoria (Australia) to appreciate the power of erosion (Plate 9). Earthquakes often create cliffs along fault lines. Rivers and ocean waves sculpt cliffs along their margins and landslide erosion often creates cliffs as well. Even man-made mine tailings can be deposited in piles with steep edges that resemble cliffs. In other words, cliffs and rock outcrops represent exposed rock surfaces of many types of disturbances. Understanding their biology assists in the restoration of similar outcrops caused by human actions.

Cliff erosion can be so infrequent that one thinks of cliffs as permanent features of a landscape. Yet, like a dormant volcano that suddenly comes to life perhaps only once in a human lifetime, cliffs inevitably erode. Talus slopes grow larger as the cliff face becomes shorter. Large rock falls may occur only when sufficiently undercut by daily, seemingly inconsequential erosive forces. Such sudden collapses can trigger tsunamis in the ocean or block and/or alter river courses. The chronic minor erosion keeps the rock faces relatively free of vegetation.

### 4.4   LESSONS FROM INFERTILE, STABLE HABITATS

Lavas and cliffs both present difficult challenges for plants, yet each offers great beauty and enhances landscape diversity. Both are stable habitats with few nutrients and frequent droughts. For vegetation to develop, both require surface heterogeneity to trap nutrients, water and seeds. Development on cliffs is also challenged by gravity, which limits the accumulation of organic matter. Cliffs may remain stable for decades, only to be eroded in one large event. Recovery on these natural surfaces is slow because the surface must be broken down and safe-sites, crucial for pioneer seed plants, must develop. Human-created land-scapes such as abandoned paved roads and urban embankments often require restoration. Whether level, sloped or vertical, restoration requires the creation of suitable cracks and protrusions.

BIBLIOGRAPHY

*Volcanoes*

Francis, P. (1995). *Volcanoes, a Planetary Perspective*. New York: Oxford University Press.
Krafft, M. (1991). *Volcanoes: Fire from the Earth*. London: Thames and Hudson Ltd.
Scarth, A. (1999). *Vulcan's Fury: Man Against the Volcano*. New Haven: Yale University Press.
Thornton, I. (1996). *Krakatau: The Destruction and Reassembly of an Island Ecosystem*. Cambridge, MA: Harvard University Press.
Winchester, S. (2003). *Krakatoa, the Day the World Exploded: August 27, 1883*. New York: Harper Collins Publishers.


*Cliffs*

Larson, D.W., Matthes, U. & Kelly, P.E. (2000). *Cliff Ecology: Pattern and Process in Cliff Ecosystems*. Cambridge: Cambridge University Press.

# 5

## Fertile and unstable habitats

### 5.1 INTRODUCTION

Not all disturbances cause a loss of fertility. Disturbances typically include events that cause a loss of biomass (plant and animal tissues, or merely some organic matter). However, disturbances can also involve the displacement of biomass across the landscape. When biomass floats downstream, the areas where that biomass is deposited can become more fertile than they were before the disturbance. Ocean currents, tides and storm surges, and the seasonal turnover of lake waters also redistribute biomass and nutrients. Many civilizations have depended on such redistribution of nutrients. River floodplains have supported mighty cultures in Egypt along the Nile and in western Asia along the Tigris and Euphrates and still periodically fertilize many agricultural hotspots with organic and mineral-rich sediments. Coastal cultures have long depended on the bountiful products of cold, upwelling ocean currents that bring nutrient-rich waters to coastlines such as Peru and Norway.

This chapter explores how humans interact with fertile, unstable habitats after sudden or chronic disasters. These habitats include unstable slopes that result in landslides, river floodplains, lakeshores and estuaries. Landslides may be hard to farm and build on, but the burgeoning human population and increasingly sophisticated building technology have led to intensive human activities, both urban and agricultural, in these habitats. It is appreciated that living on a floodplain carries dangers, but floodplains are among the most fertile agricultural sites. Thus, while humans would prefer to live on stable sites that do not flood, they often rely on floods to deposit nutrients on their fields. Floodplains are also easy to develop and close to transportation links, so many cities have grown dramatically on flood-prone sites. As populations increase, the impacts of disturbances increase. Lakes are

---

**Box 5.1  A landslide dams a stream**

Clambering over waterlogged tree trunks and mossy rocks, Lawrence hurries to keep up with his host who effortlessly scales the steep greywacke slopes from the mountain stream to measure another beech forest plot. A magnitude 6.7 earthquake in 1994 shook these ancient beech forests in central New Zealand and caused numerous landslides. One blocked this particular stream, creating a temporary pond. Eventually the stream burst the dam, but not before many nearby trees had died. Escaping death by gravity, they died from flooding (Fig. 5.1).

---

normally stable in a human time frame, but in today's water-starved world, they are in global retreat. Estuaries and marshes are also normally stable, but development, alteration of river patterns and siltation are also taking a toll on these habitats. Because these coastal ecosystems are a major defense against powerful storms, when disasters occur the damage becomes intensified. We will identify where lessons learned from natural recovery processes can help humans minimize losses of property and lives while continuing to exploit the benefits of occasional inputs of nutrients from biomass movement on unstable surfaces.

## 5.2  LANDSLIDES

### 5.2.1  Introduction

Landslides seem to happen with increasing frequency, but their impact on ecosystems and human affairs is not widely appreciated. They are the sudden downhill movement of soil or rock that is triggered mainly by earthquakes, volcanic eruptions, prolonged rains or undercutting (e.g. by water erosion or road construction; Box 5.1; Fig. 5.1). Other processes such as freeze–thaw cycles, loss of stabilizing vegetative cover (e.g. due to grazing, logging, hurricane damage), disruption of topographic features by geological uplift, and scouring by glaciers or wind erosion also cause slope failure. Landslides vary in size from localized slumps less than $15\,m^2$ to enormous underwater landslides more than $1{,}500\,km^2$, as on the slopes of the Hawaiian island chain. Such underwater landslides often generate tsunamis. Mudflows and dirty avalanches (which move soil and rocks along with snow) are other variations of potentially massive movement of soil and rock. Smaller-scale movement can occur on inclined surfaces such as road

Fig. 5.1 A landslide (in foreground) from a magnitude 6.7 earthquake blocked the Avoca River (New Zealand), causing a temporary pond that drowned the trees in the center of the photo (see Box 5.1). Landslides can quickly alter the landscape.

cuts, dikes, landscaping retention walls, trails and ski slopes. Steep, soil-free slopes such as mine tailings and rocky cliffs are far less fertile than landslides, although the amount of fertile topsoil that remains on a landslide is highly variable. In this section, we explore some basic geology of landslides, human interactions with landslides and general principles for rehabilitating them using a successional framework. Can we learn how to stabilize landslides using knowledge of succession?

### 5.2.2   Physical setting

Landslides are most common on steep, unstable surfaces such as soils with high sand content or where rainfall is high, such as on tropical mountains. However, landslides are ubiquitous, affecting an estimated one percent of the earth's surface. In highly erosive areas, with high rainfall or rapid geological uplift, up to 7.5 percent of the surface can be affected by landslides at any given time. For example, coastal temperate areas with mountains that intercept moist winds from the ocean (British Columbia, Chile, New Zealand, Norway) have temperate rain forests. Where these forests occur on steep slopes, trees often survive only several hundred years before they are toppled by landslides (Fig. 5.2). On the South Island of New Zealand, the Australian Plate

Fig. 5.2  Landslides on steep slopes in northern Colombia. Landslides dot
the Andes and other high mountains, showing how important this type of
disturbance is to mountain landscapes in earthquake prone areas.
(Courtesy of Eduardo Velázquez Martín.)

pushes against the Pacific Plate and the mountains are lifted 1 cm per
year. This leads to very active erosion, as the South Island is eroded into
the Pacific Ocean (Fig. 5.3). Mt. Cook, the highest mountain in New
Zealand, actually lost 10 m in 1991 due to a landslide, and Mt. Rainier
(Washington, USA) lost several hundred meters when the peak collapsed
under its own weight at about 5,600 BP.

Landslides can occur in relatively dry or flat terrain if a slope is
sufficiently destabilized. Intense, short rainfall typically produces shallow landslips while prolonged rainfall can trigger deeper soil saturation
and larger debris flows. Either way, there is often a minimal threshold of
amount and intensity of rain that will cause the slope to destabilize.
In Puerto Rico, that threshold is about 100 mm of rain per hour for
one hour, 10 mm of rain per hour for 10 hours or 1 mm of rain per hour
for 100 hours.

Layers of heavy, saturated soils on the surface may slip at the
interface with unweathered bedrock below. Movement of bedrock or
soil can be by rotational slumps that produce concave surfaces or planar
slides parallel to the ground. In both, the original layers remain intact.
In contrast, debris flows mix the eroded materials as they tumble down
slope. The most rapid movements are generally from falling rock or
undercutting of soil, although debris flows can be extremely rapid.

Fig. 5.3 A landslide draining into the Otira River in Arthur's Pass (New Zealand). This is one of many landslides in the Southern Alps of central South Island, New Zealand where tectonic uplift causes high erosion rates.

Often slopes will creep slowly for years, and then collapse. Recurrence of landslides is typical until the slope has eroded back to the top of the ridge. This process may take only one landslide event or many centuries of intermittent erosion.

Stabilization and regeneration of landslides should address the anatomy of a landslide scar. Landslides typically leave an upper slip face or head scarp (Fig. 5.4a), a scour zone or chute in the middle of the landslides (Fig. 5.4b) and a deposition zone at the base (foot) of the landslide (Fig. 5.4c). Chutes can be truncated or up to several kilometers long. Slip faces and deposition zones can range in area from tiny to huge. Removal of the deposition zone by river erosion or by humans with bulldozers can trigger further slope destabilization.

### 5.2.3    Landslides in the lives of humans

Thousands of people die annually in landslides (Table 5.1). In northern China (Shanxi Province), the earthquake of 1556 caused massive

Fig. 5.4 Landslides in the Caribbean National Forest (Puerto Rico).
(a) Upper slip face, showing the steep face and undisturbed forest perched
precariously above the landslide area. (b) Central chute and slip face; this
landslide lacks a deposition zone because it slid into a river that swept all
the material away. (c) Deposition zone showing the mixture of organic
material and mineral soil that create patchy conditions for rapid
regeneration.

Fig. 5.4 (cont.)

Table 5.1. *Large and destructive landslides since 1933 in decreasing order by size (from http://www.landslides.usgs.gov).*

| Volume ($\times 10^6$ m$^3$) | Location and Cause | Date | Deaths |
|---|---|---|---|
| 2,800 | Mount St. Helens, USA (earthquake, volcanic eruption) | 1980 | 5 |
| 1,600 | Huancavelica, Peru (rainfall, river erosion) | 1974 | 450 |
| 450 | Yunnan, China (unknown) | 1965 | 444 |
| 250 | Friulivenezia-Griula, Italy (unknown) | 1963 | 2,000 |
| 200 | Papua, New Guinea (earthquake) | 1986 | None |
| >150 | Sichuan, China (earthquake) | 1933 | 9,300 |
| 75–110 | Napo, Ecuador (earthquake) | 1987 | 1,000 |
| 30–50 | Ancash, Peru (earthquake) | 1970 | 18,000 |
| 35 | Gansu, China (unknown) | 1983 | 237 |
| 27 | Cauca, Colombia (earthquake) | 1994 | 271+ |
| 21 | Utah, USA (snowmelt and heavy rain) | 1983 | None |
| 13 | Ancash, Peru (unknown) | 1962 | 5,000 |

destruction, with much of the death and destruction due to the collapse of steep cliffs where many people had cave dwellings. In contrast to earthquakes and volcanoes, which can kill tens of thousands in a single episode, landslides are small, but frequent, and affect most regions of the world. They damage property, but usually kill relatively few people in a given episode. These deaths occur without regard to climate. Flooding can be an important secondary cause of death when dams caused by landslides break.

Landslides in remote mountains are of little concern unless they impede drainage of critical watersheds or create tsunamis along ocean shores. The interface between people and landslides occurs mostly along transportation corridors and in developed areas. The magnitude 7.6 earthquake that devastated large areas of Kashmir on October 8, 2005 produced landslides that cut off roads and trails linking rural communities to supply lines and escape routes. With over 30,000 deaths from the initial collapse of buildings and slopes, and many more due to loss of shelter and access to medicine and food for survivors, this tragedy is a major natural disaster. Nothing can be done about the ultimate cause – the northward movement of the Indian tectonic plate that is pushing up the Himalayan mountain range on the Eurasian plate. However, recent improvements in earthquake prediction (using ultra-low frequency radio waves) coupled with better selection of house sites and building materials will reduce deaths from future quakes.

For centuries farmers have practiced terrace agriculture on steep slopes in Asia and Latin America in order to maximize cropland and reduce erosive landslides. However, overgrazing or a harvest poorly timed just before severe rains can cause destabilization. Modern agriculture too often features monocultures, heavy grazing along watercourses and clear cutting of forests, all factors that promote loss of topsoil, sometimes in the form of landslides.

The poor are often forced to build their homes on erosion-prone slopes, such as those found outside Caracas, Venezuela or in Rio de Janeiro, Brazil because those slopes are the only terrain left. Home construction on these slopes is unlikely to use retaining walls or pylons for stability so heavy rains often cause mortality and loss of property. Wealthy residents may choose scenic hillsides, often along a waterfront, and dismiss erosion dangers. Residents were only allowed to rebuild on a Pacific Ocean coastline in the USA where previous homes had been destroyed if they rebuilt using structural improvements that would withstand a similar force. Who can guarantee that the next landslide or mudslide will not be stronger?

Fig. 5.5 Mount St. Helens debris flow on Toutle River, initiated by the largest landslide in history. The photo was taken one year after the eruption, yet erosion had already created steep banks on the river. The lakes at bottom of view were formed when the debris blocked creeks. The lakes remain in place after 25 years.

A small earthquake on Mount St. Helens, Washington (USA) triggered the largest measured terrestrial landslide in history in 1980. The landslide released building pressure, leading to the devastating eruption discussed earlier. It covered about $60\,km^2$ and extended for $14\,km$ downstream, traveling at over $100\,km$ per hour (Fig. 5.5). It contained over $2.8\,billion\ m^3$ of material, yet the landslide killed only five people (57 people died in the eruption). The size of this event, captured on film from over $25\,km$ distance, is staggering, yet small compared to the extent of the blast force which it released. This blast covered $600\,km^2$, more than four times the size of Washington, DC.

Landslides are a natural result of geological uplift and erosive forces. In many cases, human activities have destabilized slopes and increased landslide frequency. Humans have also expanded their houses onto steep slopes as urban land becomes scarce. Therefore, humans are interacting more frequently than ever with landslides. Finding a way to live with these disturbances is critical.

Fig. 5.6 A landslide in Puerto Rico dominated by vine-like ferns (Gleicheniaceae). These and similar ferns quickly stabilize landslide surfaces throughout the tropics.

### 5.2.4 Ecological responses

Landslide recovery varies due to slope stability and fertility. Stability is influenced by the steepness of the landslide, the local geology and the vegetative cover. Fertility is impacted by general geologic factors such as surface age and type, climatic factors that govern decomposition and the distribution of organic matter, including vegetative cover. Landslides on newly exposed, rocky and largely sterile glacial moraines that are distant from vegetated areas will revegetate more slowly than nutrient rich sediments on a landslide surrounded by potential plant colonists in a wet tropical forest. Within a landslide, slip faces are usually infertile and unstable, with exposed bedrock and continued erosion. Chutes are also susceptible to major erosion events but are often less steep than the slip face. The typical narrowness of chutes reduces the distance plants and animals have to cross in order to colonize the new surfaces, so colonization can be rapid. The deposition zone of landslides is relatively stable and fertile, resulting in rapid regrowth of surviving plant fragments or rapid colonization and growth of new arrivals. However, even in the deposition zone, future erosion can reset succession.

Stabilization occurs naturally on Puerto Rican landslides when native, vine-like ferns colonize infertile surfaces with their extensive rhizomes, dense growth form and copious litter production (Fig. 5.6).

In other words, the growth form of a plant can determine its competitive success.

Two recent experiments concerning Puerto Rican landslides illustrate these ideas. In one, we kept patches of landslides clear of vine-like ferns. This meant removing a mass of live and dead intertwining fronds 1 to 2 m deep. Over an eight year period, some tree seedlings took advantage of this opportunity to establish. However, other plants capable of rapid vegetative spread (including vines, herbs, grasses and club mosses) dominated most of our plots. In the control plots, the fern cover continued to dominate, letting nothing else grow. In a second experiment, we kept fast-growing pioneer trees from invading new landslide surfaces to see if these trees facilitated the development of later successional trees (that typically grow more slowly). Instead of giving later trees a chance to grow, our experimental removals resulted in a robust invasion of vines and vine-like herbs. On control plots, tall forests of early successional trees grew unimpeded. Although eight years is not long enough for a definitive answer, we think that late successional trees will appear sooner when early successional trees precede them. Therefore, at least on unstable but fertile landslides in Puerto Rico, vine-like growth forms inhibit tree growth and delay succession. Competition can influence succession after many other types of disturbance as well, and should be incorporated into any human manipulations.

### 5.2.5   Human responses

Stabilization on steep surfaces can be promoted by several ecological and engineering techniques that vary in the degree of effort required. Ecological approaches are usually more effective than engineering ones, and are most helpful when one has a detailed understanding of local succession. There is a tradeoff between immediate cover and stabilization of exposed slides by fast-growing species, and promotion of long-term succession to provide stability.

Simple addition of fertilizer or organic mulches can often promote spontaneous vegetative growth that will stabilize landslides with a minimum of effort. More effort may be required, such as sowing rapidly growing grasses or herbs that quickly cover the slope. Vines, bamboo or early successional shrubs and trees adapted to high-light environments and ongoing soil slumping have the best chance of survival. Sometimes woody plants can be established from cuttings. Engineering efforts to stabilize landslides in Puerto Rico include

Fig. 5.9 Jute blankets cover this landslide (Puerto Rico) where some early successional plants are emerging. Engineering techniques to restore landslide vegetation sometimes promote short-term substrate stability but can also inhibit successional development for longer-term stabilization.

(in order of effort invested); silt fences, contouring, jute cloth covers, rock-filled gabions and redirection of water flow by the creation of lined alternative drainage channels (Fig. 5.9). In more urban areas, retention walls are sometimes built. However, even the most altered landscape can be vulnerable to erosion during extreme storms, especially when earthquakes or water flow destroy human barriers.

Successional dynamics on landslides can guide efforts to accelerate stabilization and revegetation and distinguish techniques designed for immediate stabilization from long-term solutions on habitats such as road verges, dirt roads and even landfills. The methods used for immediate slope stabilization can have lasting effects. Excessive fertilization or the wrong choice of plant cover can lead to competitive inhibition of later successional species by dense swards of plants. Potential benefits of middle and late successional plants include deeper root penetration contributing to greater slope stability, and more plant biomass leading to soil development.

Introduced weedy plants sometimes invade the exposed soils of landslides. Roadsides provide a common invasion corridor for weeds, that are often transported along highways by vehicles and grow well in the infertile, frequently bulldozed road verges (e.g. mullein on Hawaiian volcanoes and tick-trefoil on Puerto Rican rainforests). Some weeds then manage to invade the surrounding vegetation from either the roadsides or the landslides. The effects of weeds vary from minimal to those that can alter many ecosystem functions (e.g. nitrogen-fixers, phosphorus accumulators, flammable species that increase fire frequency). The integration of weed effects with restoration goals is possible if the impacts of a particular weed are already known. However, this is rarely the case, as weeds are spreading faster than biologists can study their impacts.

Logging, over-grazing and road building each destabilizes a slope, but by different means. Slopes can be re-stabilized by introducing species that can develop rapidly by vegetative means. Landslides demonstrate the importance of legacies in the revegetation of disturbed sites. Sites lacking survivors develop much more slowly than sites with seeds, buried plant parts and topsoil.

### 5.2.6    Links with other disturbances

Many disturbances destabilize slopes and trigger landslides. Glacial moraines collapse following erosion from melt water or wind (Fig. 5.10). Earthquakes are a principal cause of landslides, especially along uplifted fault lines, near sinkholes or on volcanoes. Other factors that permit landslides to occur include fires or hurricanes, which remove stabilizing vegetation cover, and rivers that undercut their banks. Landslides, in turn, can generate tsunamis or dam rivers to cause flooding. When a landslide crashes into a lake, a devastating flood can occur.

Human activities such as logging, mining and particularly construction of roads and buildings can facilitate landslides. Increased use of steep hillsides for urban expansion will result in more deaths and property destruction from landslides such as those that occurred in 2005 in southern California. Overgrazing (and seasonal crop production) also destabilizes slopes by removing protective ground cover.

### 5.3    RIVER FLOODPLAINS

### 5.3.1    Introduction

Rivers shape the land by carving canyons and eroding mountains. Floodplains, the banks and channels of rivers that are at least occasionally flooded, were the focus of the first western civilizations and continue to be centers of human activity. Floodplains are very practical

Fig. 5.10 A landslide formed by an eroding glacial moraine in front of the Fox Glacier (New Zealand).

places for humans to gather, with guaranteed water and flat, fertile surfaces for agriculture or building. Historically, rivers provided protection from wild animals and enemies, a source of readily available food, and corridors for transportation of crops and people and disposal of wastes. Today, rivers provide useful political boundaries, a source of recreation and, of course, are still important sources of water. The link between humans and rivers is strong.

Moving water can remove nutrients from the soil, but floodplains are relatively fertile substrates when they are bathed by nutrients from upstream sources of eroded soils. Floodplains that drain glacial moraines or other poorly developed soils can remain relatively infertile for years. Yet even harsh sites supply regular moisture for plant growth.

Along with the advantages of fertility come the dangers of instability. Flood frequency and severity determine which plants can survive and which plant communities can develop on a given floodplain. Floods frequently cause destruction of crops, roads, homes and businesses. The more engineering that is done to control a river's path, the greater are the floods when they burst the barriers — as they always do, eventually.

---

**Box 5.2  Tricky passages**

Slipping on the tumbling rocks, Lawrence links arms with a buddy to make it safely across a flood-swollen and icy New Zealand river. Each day Lawrence traverses the river 5–10 times to visit plots that might disappear at any time. In fact, one day he came back to find some of the plots gone – buried under 5 m of huge rocks from one of the many floods that regularly erode this zone of rapid geologic uplift (1 cm/yr). Wet boots are a minor annoyance compared with losing so many plots. Natural disasters are to be expected on flood-plains but further insult came when a backhoe, extracting the huge rocks for road construction, damaged many of his remaining plots.

---

Floodplains come in all sizes, from occasional beaches along a narrow slot canyon wall to the immense deltas that form at the mouths of large rivers such as the Amazon, Mississippi or Nile. Floodplain surfaces can be rocky, sandy, silty or muddy, typically reflecting the geology of their surroundings. In this section we will look at the diversity of types of floodplains, how they have shaped human history, and what they offer in terms of natural resources and explore how humans interact with and manipulate the processes of recovery following disturbance on floodplains.

### 5.3.2  Physical setting

Floodplains are highly variable, changing spatially from the source to the mouth of each river and changing in time as floods come and go, triggered by seasonal melt water or storms. Some floodplains (and their accompanying rivers) are extremely short. One very short river on the Oregon (USA) coast is less than 100 m long before it joins the ocean. In contrast, major rivers such as the Nile (Africa; 6,611 km), Amazon (South America; 6,400 km), Yangtze (China; 6,264 km), Ob-Irtysh (Russia; 5,379 km), Mississippi (North America; 3,705 km) and Danube (Europe; 2,841 km) drain whole continents.

All rivers have a watershed, the land that drains into the river and its many tributaries. The geological composition and rate of geological uplift in the watershed determines the type and degree of erosion of the river and the chemical composition of the water and adjacent floodplain (Box 5.2). The amount and seasonality of rainfall determines the flow. These factors produce an astounding array of floodplains. Rivers erode basaltic columns in blocks, often forming lovely waterfalls, as in Iceland. Rivers in limestone create sinkholes and caves as well as karst hills, as in

---

**Box 5.3  Up the river**

Thirty gallons of gas and two propellers were barely enough for
Lawrence's motorboat adventure up the Grand Canyon from Lake
Mead. After passing exquisitely colored rocks set at odd angles and
God's Pocket (a lovely cove for swimming on a hot day), Lawrence
and his companions left the flat waters of Lake Mead and entered
the canyon. At one spot high above in a limestone layer there was an
old cable crossing the river on which a miner had hauled his
unusual treasure of bat guano across. In the same spot there was
also a rare bear poppy plant. Reaching a rapid current, Lawrence
tried to follow the other boat but the propeller scraped against a
hard bottom, shearing most of all three blades completely off.
Struggling to make it to the shore, he replaced the propeller with
his spare one. A lava dike, the resistant remnant of a lava flow that
had once blocked the mighty Colorado River, had done the damage.
The erosive forces of the river had (mostly) cleared the channel.

---

southern China or northwestern Puerto Rico. Sandstones can erode into
steep, narrow slot canyons as in the southwestern USA. Mixtures of rock
types can be highlighted when water erodes one type, but not another,
forming overhanging cliffs, narrow chutes, remnant boulders and other
features. Although floodplains' size, shape and stability are determined
by the dynamics of the watershed, their locations have historical
explanations. Many rivers follow ancient channels from huge inland
lakes to the ocean. Sometimes these lakes resulted from glacial melt
water. Lake Bonneville (Utah; 52,000 km$^2$ – about the size of Costa Rica)
and Lake Lahontan (Nevada; 20,700 km$^2$ – about the size of Israel)
reached their maximum extent around 12–15 K BP, during the end of
the most recent ice age. Lake Bonneville emptied precipitously from Red
Rock Pass in Idaho into the Snake River basin in a flood that may have
lasted an entire year. Other rivers have kept their channels for millions
of years, continuously cutting down into successive layers of uplifted
rock. Most rivers have their channels blocked occasionally, sometimes
by landslides or even lava flows. If the channel is well incised, the
obstruction is quickly removed (see Box 5.3)

Floodplains alongside rivers in steep terrain are often poorly
developed, narrow and ephemeral. They are most well developed on
relatively flat terrain where rivers carry high sediment loads and are
subject to periodic flooding beyond the normal channel (Fig. 5.11).
Frequent sediment deposition occurs at the boundary between steep

Fig. 5.11 Old meanders of the Kokatahi River, western South Island
(New Zealand). The active channel frequently moves across the floodplain,
so vegetation can establish when erosion ceases for several years.

and flat terrain, where water currents quickly slow down. Meandering
rivers may have floodplains that are many kilometers wide (e.g.
Bangladesh). Flood frequency helps influence floodplain succession
and human use of the land.

### 5.3.3   Floodplains in the lives of humans

Humans and floodplains have a long, intimate history. Rivers were the
easiest way for humans to explore new continents, especially where
vegetation was dense, as in central Africa, or where mountains were
rugged, as in the western USA or central Asia. Floodplains were the
campsites of early travelers and later became trading posts, then
villages. Big cities have grown up around the convenience provided by
shipping access to the ocean, fertile pastures and gardens nearby and a
steady water supply. The Nile River supported millennia of rich Egyptian
culture and later became the route used by German and English
explorers into the interior of Africa, seeking its source. The Vikings are
most famous for their forays along Europe's coasts but less well known
are their adventures along river corridors from Scandinavia through
Russia and all the way to Constantinople (modern Istanbul, Turkey). The
trappers of North America used rivers to find new beaver territories,
trapping most of the beaver from floodplains in central and western
North America between about 1650 and 1850. Gold miners also used

rivers on many continents (such as the Yukon in Alaska, USA) to reach their mining sites. Ore was then sieved from the floodplain sediments. Hydraulic mining rips up the riverbed, reshaping the floodplain. Geologists value rivers because the eroded profiles display obvious layers of earth's history. John Wesley Powell, a one-armed adventurer and geologist, was strapped to a chair in his boat while his comrades paddled on the first documented trip down the Grand Canyon in the USA. Landing on the occasional sandbar, Powell would somehow climb the cliffs with his one arm in order to study the 1.25 billion years of rock formations they passed through.

In modern times, humans have continued to use rivers for transport, natural resources, irrigation, flood control, power generation, recreation and waste disposal. Even today, most journeys in dense rainforests throughout the tropics are made by water. Roads and trails, where they exist, have to be maintained constantly lest they be quickly overgrown. In contrast, rivers remain open corridors for travel. Barges ply many large rivers, often depending on dredges to keep shifting sandbars under control. Artificial rivers (canals) have facilitated movement of trade goods and people by connecting oceans to each other (Panama Canal and Suez Canal) and oceans to interiors (Erie Canal from the Atlantic Ocean across the Appalachian Mountains to Lake Erie in North America). Many canals in western Europe, built for commerce, are now prime tourist attractions. For example, one can float down the Canal du Rhône in luxury, stopping at many lovely towns of the French *Midi*, such as Castelnaudary or Toulouse.

Rivers still supply most humans with a steady water supply and fertile floodplains for agriculture. Farmers tolerate minor floods but object to disastrous flooding, especially when infertile gravels are deposited or erosion removes fertile soil. It is convenient to forget that the land itself was a result of flooding and will continue to be reshaped over time. Rivers and their floodplains also continue to be important habitats for fish such as salmon, trout, Amazonian catfish and many more. Less exploited rivers, such as the Kamchatka River, Russian Far East, are major habitats for many species and serve as baselines for the restoration of degraded rivers.

Humans have diverted rivers for irrigation since the beginning of agriculture over 10,000 years ago. The Tigris and Euphrates Rivers were tamed by Sumerians more than 6,000 years ago using levees (raised banks of earth) and irrigation canals. The resulting stable food supply permitted the explosion of civilization, but also initiated disastrous consequences. Because of limited rainfall in this Mesopotamian region, salinization gradually overcame agriculture because water evaporated from the fields rather than draining from them. In addition, the two rivers carry high silt loads. As a result, the region became the desert it is today, with poor agricultural land, droughts alternating with floods and chronic soil salinity. Incidentally, the Sumerian epic poem "Gilgamesh" is based in part on catastrophic floods in this region, and probably forms the context for the account of Noah and the flood in Genesis. Much later, the Abbasid caliphate renovated these water management systems during the great Islamic expansion. The riches of Baghdad that resulted ultimately sustained Islam through the five Christian crusades. However, by the early thirteenth century, the system again collapsed due to salinization and a massive flood that wrecked the system. Iraq has not yet recovered.

The Nile River was tamed by the Pharaohs in a way that sustained agriculture for millennia. Floods are benign because Egypt is far from the source, but the Nile did flood consistently during the summer over a period of three months. This gentle gift was turned into a great civilization. The abundance of water helped to stem salinization and deposited nutrients annually. Today, over 95 percent of Egyptians live near the Nile, on about 2 percent of the country's area. However, the High Dam at Aswan has tamed the Nile, and the river no longer floods. While electrical power is generated, the lake is silting rapidly. Egypt's agriculture no longer receives its annual supplement of silt and the fisheries of the eastern Mediterranean have suffered due to the lack of nutrients which were once brought to the sea.

Roman aqueducts (Latin *aqua*, "water," and *ducere*, "to lead") were a marvel of the ancient world. Certainly, Rome and the larger cities could not be sustained. Builders used tunnels, inverted siphons and the familiar arched bridges to transport sweet spring water, free of pollution, to their baths and fountains. The first aqueduct, the Aqua Appia, was built in 312 BC. By AD 226, the Romans had built 11 aqueducts just to serve Rome. Romans used good ecological intuition to find springs (e.g. green grass in summer, wetland plants where water was not obvious). While the emperors and the rich commanded a large portion of the water, public fountains were fed from huge cisterns so that people were always near water. The importance of this water was reflected during medieval times when most of the aqueducts had ceased to function and water came from the Tiber River. This enormously constricted the population of Rome and caused widespread disease. During the Renaissance, aqueducts and fountains were revived and the city flourished once again.

Irrigation was also crucial in the development of American civilizations. Near the northern coast of Peru, in the Zaña Valley, old buried canals were recently revealed. These canals, lined with stone, carried water from the mountains to irrigate crops of cotton, beans and squash as early as 6,700 years ago, eventually leading to the development of an integrated community, a bureaucracy and large urban areas. By 5,000 years ago, other Peruvian centers in arid regions were thriving due to irrigation technology.

Normal, unaltered floodplains absorb periodic floods and recover. However, human encroachment on floodplains for agriculture and cites has made us vulnerable to damage from the normal cycles of flooding and increased the severity of the floods that occur. The desire to have a steady supply of water for irrigation as well as the desire for flood control leads to the construction of dams and levees. The Mississippi River is lined for much of its length by levees to channel its flow. This manipulation creates problems when floodwaters breach the levees. Then normally dry homes, city streets and fields are suddenly inundated. The potential for destruction was demonstrated following Hurricane Katrina in August 2005, when the storm surge breached levees to flood much of New Orleans (Louisiana, USA).

Flowing water has long powered human industries with a cheap, renewable source of energy. Grinding flour and pumping water into homes and irrigation channels were early uses of river water. Turning turbines to generate electricity is the most common modern use of rivers. Large dams such as the Aswan Dam (Egypt) or Hoover Dam (USA) increase the efficiency and constancy of power supplies, increase travel safety and provide reservoirs for human recreation, but dramatically alter flood regimes and the flora and fauna adapted to seasonal flooding.

Recreational uses of rivers and their floodplains range from sedate float trips down canals of western France to wild jet boat rides on many New Zealand rivers. Fishers seek solitude fly-fishing in Wyoming and adventure trying to catch salmon in Kamchatka. Ecotourism is supported by raft trips on Siberian rivers and by luxurious cruises on the Amazon River. Tidal bores (tidal waves that come up rivers) attract tourists to rivers in Nova Scotia, Alaska and elsewhere. The world's strongest tidal bore occurs during the full moon in the Qiantang River in the Zhejiang Province (China). Surfers even ride these waves upriver. Riverfronts can host fish markets, restaurants, beaches and retirement homes. Most humans are never far from water.

---

**Box 5.4  Not like it used to be**

Canteens were mostly optional for Lawrence as a young boy hiking in Vermont with the Plainfield Rangers — for hot days or high ridges. Every creek was a chance to lie down on the mossy rocks and drink the cold, refreshing water. Twenty years later, Lawrence had to train his young sons to use portable filters or iodine pills; just to have a sip of free-flowing water meant the risk of getting giardia. Today there are a few remote watersheds in New Zealand, a few mountain springs in Nevada and a few creeks in Alaska where Lawrence still savors the belly slurp of clean, safe water. How long will it be until these special places also are polluted?

---

Rivers are the circulatory system of the land, reflecting land use and land abuse. A city with a clear, clean river running through it has successfully managed its wastes. Unfortunately, clean rivers are rare and usually associated with areas of very low human population density. Just 40 years ago, one could safely drink from most woodland creeks in the continental USA. Today most waterways in the world are too contaminated to drink without treatment (Box 5.4).

River floodplains are efficient waste disposal systems when used in moderation. Wastes are filtered, diluted, mixed and aerated, then digested and absorbed by microorganisms, plants and animals. Some nutrient addition can fertilize downstream agriculture. Unfortunately, most river floodplains are subjected to more waste than they can handle. Further, industrial use of rivers has increased, with occasional catastrophic results. The Cuyahoga River in Cleveland, Ohio (USA) actually burned in 1969 because it had become so polluted. Power plants that use river water to cool their turbines release heated water that kills many organisms. Mining effluents can lace rivers with very toxic wastes. A worst-case incident occurred in November 2005 when the Heilong (Amur in Russia) River in China became polluted by benzene from an explosion at a chemical plant in Jilin Province. The 600,000 residents of the Russian city of Khabarovsk had to depend on newly drilled wells for fresh water until the waste had passed downstream.

Pollution of most waterways in the world is cause for alarm. Costs for water treatment, health costs for those who become ill from drinking untreated water, and clean-up costs for industrial accidents are burdening national economies. Opportunities for employment and financial savings lie in restoring floodplains to a healthier state.

### 5.3.4   Ecological responses

There are many alternative ways for vegetation to develop following flooding, depending on the fertility and stability of the floodplain.
The disturbance regime determines the stability of the floodplain and
sets the boundaries of any response by plants or animals. The dispersal
of these plants and animals onto the floodplain is a key component of
the biotic response to flooding. Dispersal is, in turn, modified by the
fertility and use of the adjacent land. Does the river flow from a nearly
sterile glacial moraine or a fertile agricultural area? Does the river flow
through a native forest, native grassland, grazed prairie or urban
wasteland? Seeds from local plants will be more likely to arrive and
germinate than seeds from more distant plants.

Annual patterns of high and low water, combined with occasional
large floods, constitute the disturbance regime of a floodplain.
Floodplain succession is finely tuned to these more or less predictable,
seasonal changes in water level. In North America, for example, widely
dispersed willow and poplar seeds cover moist riverbanks just as high
waters recede. Viable for only days, the maturation and dispersal of
these seeds is carefully synchronized with seasonal flooding. These early
colonists help to stabilize the riverbank and promote accumulation of
sediments by retarding the flowing water, causing suspended sediments
to precipitate. As sediments accumulate to form higher river bars,
later successional, less flood-tolerant species such as alder, maple, ash or
spruce are able to establish (Fig. 5.12). Many such species have water-
dispersed seeds and are left behind by floodwaters. In non-forested
habitats, sturdy grasses and reeds that can survive both inundation and
drought often predominate because water levels fluctuate throughout
the year. Severe floods periodically reset the successional process on
floodplains.

### 5.3.5   Human responses to damage along riparian corridors

Restoration of riparian corridors may be enhanced by prior analysis of
the flood regimes relative to native species. Biodiversity may be
enhanced directly through sowing and planting desirable species,
by initiating successional processes or by reestablishing connections
along the corridor. Removal of dams for economic or ecological reasons
allows study of the recovery of plants and animals adapted to the
seasonal flooding and occasional severe floods that scour the floodplain.
Lowering of water levels in reservoirs upstream from dams due to

Fig. 5.12 Establishment of later successional spruce trees (background) is possible on floodplains (in central Alaska) only when terrace levels build up sufficiently to avoid frequent erosion. The foreground is dominated by young willows that are inundated every few years.

drought or management decisions also allows examination of colonization dynamics without flooding disturbance. Periodic releases of flood-level volumes of water from dams can imitate natural floods and have ecological consequences. In an attempt to reestablish habitat for rare fish, reduce cover of non-native tamarisk trees and increase beach habitat for recreational boaters, experimental releases of high water flows from the Glen Canyon Dam into the Grand Canyon (southwestern USA) have been conducted since 2003. Impacts of these floods are still being evaluated but the early indications are that they have had some success. Yet most releases from dams are based on needs of downstream water users (especially farmers), not the needs of rare plants and animals. Annual fluctuations of 5–20 meters in Lake Mead and Lake Mohave below the Grand Canyon have favored invasion of tamarisk trees (Fig. 5.13; Plate 10) at the cost of reproduction of native willows and poplars. Slight changes in timing of water releases that would allow regeneration of native trees could be made if there were enough political emphasis put on restoration.

Rivers have been major avenues for exploration (i.e. the desperate Amazon voyage of Francisco de Orellana in 1540–41 and the epic journey of the Corps of Discovery led by Lewis and Clark). Rivers also provide excellent avenues for the invasive species that soon follow the

Fig. 5.13 The drawdown zone of Lake Mead, in the Colorado River, USA. Scant vegetation can colonize the fluctuating margin of most reservoirs in dry climates. (Courtesy of Willard E. Hayes, II.)

explorers. Often scoured on an annual basis, floodplains provide a moist growing environment relatively free of competition. Plant dispersal is aided by downstream and downhill water flow and by winds that funnel up or cold air that settles down into river valleys. Gallery forests, forests along streams, are common in both wet and dry climates and provide cover for animal dispersal. The favored willows planted in the USA are weeds in pastoral New Zealand, where they grow so vigorously that they desiccate streams for much of the year. New Zealand floodplains are also beset by weeds of European (Scotch broom) or Asian (butterfly bush) origin, that permanently alter habitats for slower-growing native plants. Ornamentals such as Chinese wisteria and Russian olive have escaped to become major problems along rivers in North America, while buck-thorns can invade many habitats including riparian zones in cooler regions of North America.

### 5.3.6  Links with other disturbances

Floodplains are the drainage channels of the landscape. Each river reflects the stability and successional status of its watershed. Young rivers pouring out of melting glaciers have nearly barren floodplains dominated by coarse boulders. Mature rivers may have gentle currents, many meanders, and mostly forested floodplains, with only occasional sand bars on the inside of meanders to hint at past flood events. All types of floodplains eventually flood by definition, but certain events trigger flooding. When glaciers, landslides or lava flows block rivers, flooding becomes a concern for downstream residents. Heavy rains that can induce flooding often accompany hurricanes and tornadoes. Grazing and logging along riverbanks or in steep watersheds cause erosion, subsequent flooding and siltation of rivers. Drying up of rivers is another form of disruption for the plants and animals of the floodplain as well as human users of the ecosystem. Floods and drought are quite closely linked. Any disruption of vegetation in the watershed reduces the water-holding capacity of the soil. Instead of the remarkably even flow one sees from an undisturbed watershed days after the most recent rain, rain-water tends to rush immediately downriver in disturbed watersheds, leaving the soils dry. As noted earlier, rivers and their floodplains are sensitive gauges of the degree of environmental degradation. The record of polluted, depleted and otherwise altered river floodplains left by humans on this planet does not bode well for our future water security.

## 5.4    LAKESHORES

### 5.4.1    Introduction

The boundary between land and lakes is usually stable, but there are catastrophic exceptions. Lakes rarely expand and usually they shrink. The causes are varied. Global warming is melting permafrost and lakes drain away. Water is diverted for many reasons, and shorelines recede. As water levels change, vegetation responds. In this section, we describe mechanisms by which vegetation normally invades lakes during primary succession. We then describe how lakes are shrinking at rates that greatly exceed the rate of succession. Finally, we ask, what lessons from normal succession might be applied to restoration around shrunken lakes?

### 5.4.2    Physical settings

Lakes and their associated vegetation are as variable as the settings within which they are found. We will concentrate on larger lakes in three climate regimes: boreal, dry temperate zones and deserts. Most lakes are filled with freshwater, but in arid regions, they gradually

Fig. 5.14  Emerald Lakes from the summit of Red Crater at 1886 m
(Tongariro National Park, New Zealand). The lakes exhibit a brilliant
greenish color because of minerals that were leached from the thermal area
along with rising steam. This region is the heart of a World Heritage Site
that attracts thousands of ecotourists annually. (Courtesy of Shane Hona.)

become saline. Problems surrounding fresh water and saline lakes (often
called "seas") differ substantially.

Boreal lakes are commonly associated with bogs. Once it was
thought that all lakes gradually filled with bogs, and eventually became
upland forests. Today, it is clear that most lake–bog complexes are in a
stable equilibrium, and that changes in vegetation only occur if water
levels change dramatically. Where succession does occur, it is not to
uplands, but to different types of wetlands (e.g. spruce swamps).

Shallow lakes often fill in during the process of primary succession. In highlands, lakes may be affected by many impacts, including
human trampling and landslides. Lakes associated with volcanism,
such as in Yellowstone National Park and many locations in New
Zealand (Fig. 5.14), provide unique habitats for the study of succession.
Lakes perched on sand dunes also demonstrate classic zonation features
described during the early years of ecology (Fig. 5.15). Typically, succession leads from open water through various communities dominated by
herbs or shrubs to forested uplands (Plate 11). In dry temperate climates,
lakes with gentle shores may gradually be filled in as vegetation

Fig. 5.15 Small lakes can form on sand dunes (Miller Woods, Indiana Dunes National Lakeshore, Indiana). This freshwater lake supports typical vegetation zonation, and is the home of several rare species of plants and butterflies.

advances along the margins. This vegetation traps sediment and the lake bottom is gradually built up. These changes are always slow on the human time scale. However, if there are rapid and major changes to the hydrology, upland vegetation does develop quickly. One situation in which changes occur rapidly is with the removal of a dam. This will result in rapid succession on the dry, exposed terrain. Warmer soils and abundant seed sources in the surrounding uplands promote rapid colonization by the available flora. Wind-dispersed species, common in riparian zones, dominate this invasion, resulting in some type of wooded vegetation.

Lakes in arid zones are particularly fragile. The hydrological regime can be disrupted by diversion of sources or by pumping directly from the lake. Evaporation hastens water loss. As lakes shrink to reveal barren shorelines, evaporation forms salty crusts. Therefore, invasion by plants becomes nearly impossible.

### 5.4.3   Lakes in the lives of human

Around the world, from Alaska to Africa and from Australia to Central Asia, lakes are drying up, whether the lake is in an arid zone or in the boreal regions. In arid regions, they are also getting saltier, leaving behind desolate borders of salty deserts as they shrink. They shrink from increasing demand (urban and agricultural) and from inefficient use. They shrink because water evaporates and, as temperatures rise, still more water evaporates. Fresh water is increasingly scarce and many analysts predict that water, not oil, will be the subject of future conflicts.

Lakes in the North American and Siberian boreal regions are disappearing. The permafrost that forms an impermeable barrier to water flow is thawing due to global warming and, as this occurs, water simply seeps away. This drying out is having a major impact on wildlife, but is thought to also lead to an acceleration of warming trends as peat is exposed and begins to decompose, releasing carbon dioxide and other greenhouse gasses into the atmosphere. In Siberia 1,200 lakes greater than 40 ha have disappeared since 1971, as tracked by satellite images. Northern lakes, where permafrost remains intact, have grown, but most of the shrinkage of lakes has been in southern Siberia. While Russian scientists seek to explain these changes as merely a consequence of normal primary succession, the rate of change massively exceeds that of succession.

Warm climates are also experiencing major lake shrinkage, but obviously for different reasons. Beautiful Lake Chapala, the largest lake in Mexico, is shrinking. Not only does this lake support many migratory and rare waterfowl, it also hosts endemic fish species. Of course, many know this lake as a retirement and tourism center essential to the economy of the central Pacific region of Mexico. In this basin, inefficient water use, increasing agriculture and irrigation, industrialization and urbanization have all taken their toll. Since 1980, the lake has been in general decline, and since 1990, when Guadalajara increased its municipal and industrial use, the decline has accelerated. Between 1986 and 2001, the lake shrank by 25,000 ha. You could fit Washington, D.C. into the newly exposed shoreline and have room left over. Water levels dropped about 3 m and water now rarely flows through its outlet. This means that agricultural chemicals, heavy metals and organic matter are all accumulating. The fisheries are declining and the shores are becoming saline. This is but one example of a global problem.

Even in temperate zones, lakes and some impoundments are desiccating as the balance between input and use is upset and as evaporation increases. Lake Powell, on the Colorado River, is shrinking due to a persistent drought and expanding water use. Boat ramps do not reach the lake and resorts are distant from water. This creates a ring of barren land subject to erosion and only slow invasion by plants, mainly wind-dispersed ones. As this impoundment of the Glen Canyon Dam is drawn down, some hope it will never be replenished and the original beauty of the canyon will be restored.

One of the greatest continuing environmental disasters is the receding shore of the Aral Sea (Uzbekistan, Kazakhstan) where only 40 years ago fishing villages thrived. Today it is impossible to see the water from those same villages. The principal rivers that fed the sea were diverted to grow cotton in a desert. What was once the world's fourth largest inland sea is now almost entirely desert. Salt coats the shores, and winds create salt storms (not sandstorms) that reach the Himalayas and coat surviving farms. Flushing salts leads to high levels of pesticides and fertilizer in the Aral Sea. Drinking water is polluted with pesticides, salt and fertilizer, so diseases are very common. Rusty hulks of fishing boats are scattered throughout the region, and fish are rare. Restoration will require decades, if it is at all possible, but current estimates are that the Aral Sea will disappear within 15 years.

Lake Chad, once Africa's fourth largest lake, has shrunk from about the size of Rwanda or Lake Erie in North America to one-twentieth of this size in 40 years. Over 20 million people live near its shores, within the West African countries of Chad, Niger, Nigeria and Cameroon. As populations increase, the lake shrinks in the face of overgrazing that removes vegetation and increases aridity. Unsustainable irrigation projects that divert water from the tributary rivers and the lake itself also contribute to the problem. As the lake recedes crops fail, herds die, fisheries disappear, soils become saline and poverty accelerates. Because the lake is very shallow, carpet grass has invaded much of the area, further affecting fish and rendering navigation nearly impossible. The prospect for Lake Chad and its people is grim. Africa's most endangered wetland will shrink to a completely managed puddle, not a functioning ecosystem.

### 5.4.4  Ecological responses

Lakes provide the water to sustain halos of luxuriant vegetation. When the water disappears, the vegetation structure and composition must necessarily change. A lake and its vegetation can be conceptualized as a bull's eye with concentric rings. As the lake shrinks, the rings march towards its center, each disappearing in turn until the vegetation again comes to equilibrium with the water regime. In general, the rate of this process matches the rate of water loss. However, this process is slow and in many cases stasis is more likely. Factors that cause lake water to disappear include gradual processes such as loss of glacial melt water to keep filling lakes, melting permafrost opening new drainages or river erosion that lowers outlets. Humans accelerate water loss by actively diverting water for agriculture or logging and grazing soils in the watershed that leads to less water being delivered to nearby lakes. More abrupt processes such as earthquakes that produce fissures in the lake or the collapse of a volcanic crater can also drain lakes.

Temperate North America experienced an epidemic of beaver dam failures when beavers were trapped to near extinction between 1650 and 1850. Beaver dams formed millions of ponds that trapped sediments and protected water quality. Now the invasion of plants into the former ponds is rapid, though scarcely studied. The return of vegetation to former beaver ponds follows patterns studied for primary succession surrounding small lakes, but appears to occur more rapidly. Plant dispersal is assisted by moving water, and competition is limited. Only about 10 percent of these beaver ponds have been reformed during the twentieth century, not enough to substantially alter watersheds. However, because the land is much more densely populated than in the seventeenth century, the occasional beaver dam failure has led to scores of recent human deaths.

### 5.4.5   Human response

Unlike many disasters discussed in this book, shrinking lakes usually result from slow, if inexorable, processes. In this way, the process resembles overgrazing. Restoration is as simple as it is next to impossible. Most lakes could be returned to productivity by restoring the hydrological regime, followed by proper biological interventions. However, in most places, there is no water to spare. Any solutions require large-scale, comprehensive programs. This symptom of global warming can only serve to ignite the imagination of governments that the problem is real and the crises are imminent.

The general strategy for coping with shrinking lakes revolves around wise water use. Civilizations have crashed from poor water management and today the future appears bleak. Efficient use of water, including recycling, reduced energy use and better planning of water resources can be employed to reduce drawdown of this resource. Salinization can be reduced by planting salt-tolerant shrubs (such as tamarisk), then harvesting the plants to remove salt. However, this is dangerous because many species are invasive, highly competitive and can suck up water with deep tap roots. Unless such plants are harvested frequently and removed, they can increase soil salinity. To date, biological reclamation of ultra-saline habitats in the USA has been attempted but rarely. The only available species group (the salt-cedars) tends to replace other species and accelerate desiccation of the landscape.

There are some signs of hope. The Aral Sea, once thought to be beyond hope, may have another chance. In a stunning example of triage, the Kazakhstan government, with the financial aid of the World Bank, has started to restore part of the Sea. The larger, southern portion will be sacrificed and efforts focused on the smaller northern portion where salinity and pollution may be manageable. To accomplish this, a dike will replace the existing sand berm to create a basin that may be partially filled from an incoming river. With luck, a fishery may be reestablished and climate amelioration may occur as a bonus. Dust storms may even be reduced.

### 5.4.6   Links with other disturbances

Shrinking lakes in arid environments produce barren shores. Winds carry the dry dust to form dust storms and produce dunes. In cold regions, shrinking lakes may alter thermal balances and intensify global warming. Lakes can be formed when massive earth movements block rivers. The debris flow from Mount St. Helens blocked numerous creeks to form new lakes that persist. In other cases, impoundments eventually breach the natural dam to cause floods.

### 5.5   SALT MARSHES AND MANGROVES

### 5.5.1   Introduction

Salt marshes and mangroves are often found in estuaries, which are large coastal bodies of water enclosed by land, but open to the sea. They may occur behind barrier islands, or along coastlines. Here, salt water and fresh water mix to permit very high productivity in a dynamic, tidally influenced habitat, and these relatively protected sites allow the establishment of productive ecosystems. The dynamic boundaries between land and sea are crucial to the efficient functioning of both. In temperate and warm temperate zones, these fringing wetlands are dominated by herbaceous species, though woody plants may invade more stable sites (Fig. 5.16). In subtropical and tropical habitats, salt

Fig. 5.16 Salt marshes in wide tidal flats (Tongass National Forest, Southeast Alaska). These sedge-dominated marshes experience very high tidal amplitude and produce abundant resources for waterfowl, salmon and other marine species. As global warming raises sea levels, the size of these marshes will shrink considerably.

tolerant shrubs form mangrove swamps (Plate 12), but often mangroves extend inland along rivers (Fig. 5.17). Both marshes and swamps can also form along protected shores that are not estuaries, but they require relatively quiet waters because exposed sites would soon be scoured of the substrates needed to support them.

### 5.5.2  Physical setting

Tidal salt marshes and mangroves survive well in a chronically disturbed habitat, usually within an estuary, but sometimes along relatively protected coastlines. Twice a day, the tides sweep in to flood the community, then flow out to expose vegetation to direct exposure to sun and waves. These communities have high productivity and can recover quickly from minor disturbances. However, they recover from even more damaging disturbances because soil remains intact, provided the landform remains intact. Soils harbor a significant part of the ecosystem, contain an active seed bank and usually permit the survival of underground parts.

Well-developed salt marshes occur throughout the world in such estuaries as Chesapeake Bay and Puget Sound in North America, the

Fig. 5.17 A freshwater mangrove swamp near Darwin (Northern Territory, Australia). Mangroves occur along a gradient from salty ocean shores to seasonally flooded stream banks. This type of forest, dominated by the freshwater mangrove (*Barringtonia acutangula*), is common throughout northern Australia, and southeastern Asia to Madagascar. It commonly occurs in narrow bands along tidal creeks.

Thames (UK), Milford Sound (New Zealand), the Bay of Bengal (India) and the Rio de la Plata (between Argentina and Uruguay). Globally, estuaries cover about 350,000 km² (about the size of Germany). The productivity of many salt marshes is comparable to rain forests, but much of the productivity floats to sea in the form of detritus. Salt marshes also occur on open coastlines such as the Atlantic and Gulf of Mexico coastlines of the USA and Mexico. These marshes are usually protected by barrier islands created by their own export of organic matter (detritus). The productivity of these marshes supports ocean fisheries as well as many migratory birds. Many marshes also include tidal creeks cut through the mud, "panes" (shallow muddy depressions that collect fresh water) and tidal flats where no vascular plants dominate.

Mangroves occur in warm waters from about 32 degrees to 38 degrees south latitude in every continent and on many large islands. There are eight plant families, 23 genera and up to 75 species of mangroves. These include life forms that range from small shrubs to impressive trees. Today, mangroves cover only 170,000 km$^2$. Since 1980, mangroves have been reduced by over 50 percent by dredging and conversion to aquaculture (primarily saltwater ponds used to raise shrimp). Species of mangroves are marvels of biological adaptation. Adults survive twice-daily inundation by seawater while rooted in sulfurous, anoxic mud. To transfer oxygen to the roots, many species have "pneumatophores" (Latin for "breath bearers"). These roots extend into the air and absorb oxygen through lenticels, which can take in air, but repel water. The roots have specialized internal tissue called aerenchyma that allows the diffusion of oxygen to buried roots. Other species have prop roots that serve the same function. Even more remarkable, the seeds of mangrove species germinate while still attached to the parent ("viviparity"), and are dispersed into seawater as floating seedlings. This dispersal has allowed mangroves to spread from their center of origin in the Indo-Malayan region to all tropical and subtropical waters.

### 5.5.3    Salt marshes and mangroves in the lives of humans

The sea has been a major source of sustenance for human populations throughout history. Coastal people used marshes and swamps to fulfill many needs. Large shell middens and mounds attest to the importance of this resource to pre-agricultural people. However, modern societies have only recently appreciated the importance of these habitats because many of the values are indirect and not easily quantified.

The productivity of salt marshes, even those at high latitudes, rivals that of the rainforest, and certainly exceeds that of most agricultural systems. The plants of marshes provide shelter and nursery grounds for fish and many marine organisms and the decaying plants provide a floating feast for marine life. Dense root systems absorb storm energy and protect inland sites while stabilizing the shoreline. Marshes and mangroves buffer inland areas from the erosion of waves and storm surges. Marsh vegetation resists water flow, so the energy of the ocean is harmlessly dissipated, thus reducing property damage and loss of human life from hurricanes and tsunamis.

Plants are highly productive and can absorb pollutants, thus improving commercial fisheries. Particulate pollutants are deposited in the sediment and sequestered from the food web, thus reducing the toxicity of the food chain. Both marshes and mangroves have been used to treat effluents from sewage plants to reduce the nutrient load in

Fig. 5.18 Salt marshes developing new mixtures of species. Tidelands on Willapa Bay (Washington) form a complex ecosystem on private land and the Willapa Bay National Wildlife refuge. The introduced *Spartina alterniflora* (see Box 5.6) has mixed with native eel grass species (*Zostera* spp.) and some sedges (*Carex* spp.). (Courtesy of Alan Trimble.)

coastal waters. Salt marshes foster diverse communities of fish, shell-fish, birds and sea mammals by providing food and habitat (Fig. 5.18).

Marshes and mangroves supported indigenous people. In North America, people such as the Haida (western coast of Canada) caught birds, fish and shellfish from tidal marshes. Marsh grasses provided clothing and roofing for others. In the southeastern USA, the size and frequency of shell middens demonstrates the importance of coastal resources to these people. Mangroves also have benefited traditional societies for millennia. With little apparent damage, mangroves have produced food, medicine, tannins, some fuel and construction materials (Box 5.5). Salt, once a precious commodity that was not easily obtained, was obtained from the leaf secretions of many mangrove species, for example by coastal aboriginal people in Australia.

The ecological functions of marshes are economically valuable. Many of the world's fisheries depend on coastal marshes for breeding habitat. Recreational activities in coastal wetlands contribute signifi-cant economic value, without which many retailers of outdoor equip-ment (e.g. snorkeling and diving equipment) would fail. Marshes provide

---

**Box 5.5  How the Maori used mangroves**

The Maori people of New Zealand used mangroves (Manawa) for
many purposes. Among mangrove roots, they gathered protein-rich
sea creatures such as mullet (kanae), snails (karahu), eels (tuna) and
oysters (parore tio). They also dyed flax using the tannin-rich earth
formed by mangrove leaves, leading to the traditional colors found
in skirts (piupiu). A characteristic green dye was collected from
lichens that also grew on the mangroves. Mangrove wood was used
to heat stones for the hangi (feast) and was preferred to upland
species because it is aromatic. Mangrove leaves were sometimes
used to keep fish cool on fishing trips.

---

many valuable lessons about ecological concepts. They are readily
accessible to those living near coasts in temperate zones and their
intrinsic interest makes them ideal outdoor classrooms.

The values of marshes were poorly appreciated until the mid
twentieth century. Marshes are messy, unstable places, unsuited to
development. So, especially in North America and Europe, they have
been dredged, drained, diked (for flood control and transportation),
ditched (for pastures and mosquito control) and filled to provide stable
surfaces. Roads and railroads were often constructed on raised beds
through marshes, altering hydrology and destroying them. In most
cases, these actions were legal when undertaken, and by 1970 over
50 percent of the coastal marshlands of the USA were gone, replaced by
farms, industry, airports and housing. Of course, the results have been
to reduce fisheries, biodiversity and productivity. The global decline of
most fisheries has been attributed primarily to over-exploitation, but
recovery of many fishing stocks is problematic due to the loss of
marshes.

Mangroves have also been destroyed for economic development,
making them the most endangered habitat on the planet. Shipping
channels are deepened and dredged and the wasteland of the swamp
was considered a good place to extract material for land fills. Thailand
lost over half its extensive mangrove swamps in 40 years. Areas once
protected by these swamps were among those most devastated by the
Boxing Day tsunami (2004). In the Philippines, less than 25 percent
of mangroves remained of the estimates from 1920, while in Ecuador,
up to 50 percent have been lost. Mangroves are killed when their air
roots are clogged by crude oil and when dikes or roads destroy tidal
regimes. In the developing world, these swamps contain some of the last

*Mangroves*

Very few species can withstand the stressful conditions found in mangrove swamps, so these swamps have few plant species. However, mangroves promote an abundance of mud-dwelling organisms, shelter birds, fish and invertebrates, promote siltation and protect the associated shorelines from storm surges, erosion and waves. Mangroves often protect coral reefs because they are firmly attached to the sediment by dense, extensive root systems. Over 500 bird species use mangroves on the Caribbean coast of Belize. A diverse assemblage of mammals, including endangered manatees, turtles, large lizards and even some monkey species, use mangroves. Mangroves also promote diversity in their lee and in the sea because they export huge amounts of detritus and shelter planktonic communities. For example, about 60 percent of the leaves produced in a year are dropped into the swamp. They are vital for proper functioning in tropical coastal ecosystems. Globally, mangroves sequester as much carbon into the ocean as the whole Amazon River. This function is vital to reduce carbon dioxide increases in the atmosphere.

When mangroves are heavily disturbed, succession may start with salt marsh plants such as rushes and sedges, followed by salt-tolerant grasses. Eventually, if mangroves are in the vicinity, they will be dispersed into the area and reform the community. In many cases, mangroves appear to undergo what might be called auto-succession, or merely recovery from disturbance. That is, after devastation, the same species return to recreate the community.

Some believe that mangroves are a stage of succession, facilitating the invasion of more landward species by accretion. This may occur where physical forces are weak, so that mangroves do foster further accretion. However, where accretion is not naturally favored, mangroves are self-maintaining and are usually a stable type of vegetation. They persist in the face of some disturbance, though catastrophic events such as typhoons will destroy them.

### 5.5.5  Human responses to devastation of marshes and mangroves

Where marshes and mangroves are filled and fringing forests cleared, erosion and siltation change landforms making restoration of these vegetation types nearly impossible. The predictable result, shown by events in the Indian Ocean and Caribbean Sea, is a terrible loss of life and unimaginable destruction of property during natural disasters. Restoring these ecosystems is a huge challenge but will pay economic dividends. In recognition of their value, restoration efforts have been initiated in many places, but much remains to be learned before high success rates are routinely achieved.

Recovery requires stabilization of the substrate, development of similar hydrological regimes and the presence of suitable colonizing species. All of these requirements usually occur shortly after a natural disaster, but are rarely present when it is decided to restore habitats altered by previous human activities.

Salt marsh restoration has been attempted in many places, with mixed results. The principal reason for failure is that tidal regimes do not develop as planned, so that planted species failed. When the hydrological regime is correct, often the planted species becomes too successful and precludes the desired succession to a more complex marsh. Poor dispersal, local pollution and local disturbances have all affected restoration projects. One lesson learned from successful projects is that tidal creeks should be part of the plan. Creeks provide aeration along the margins, enhance biotic diversity, promote dispersal and encourage fish populations.

Marsh restoration studies have also emphasized that different aspects of constructed marshes develop at different rates. Some measures of success, such as overall biomass and biodiversity, quickly equilibrate at levels similar to mature natural marshes. Other functional measures, such as soil organic matter and nitrogen, take much longer to achieve. Success of a project requires decades, not years, to be fairly judged.

Mangrove restoration has taken on urgency since the Indian Ocean tsunami in 2004 because damage was reduced where mangroves were dense. Proper restoration of mangroves is more difficult than that of salt marshes, though the same forces need to be considered. Tides, local hydrological patterns, predation on the seedlings and proper location (zonation patterns) are some of the controlling factors. Hypersalinity is a major problem that will reduce biomass accumulation, change the fauna and alter plant species composition.

Despite the conversion of most of its mangrove resources to other uses, the Republic of Vietnam has begun to restore some, primarily in association with the tourist market. At the Can Gio Biosphere Reserve, about $7\,km^2$ of an estuarine tidal flat are being converted into a mangrove–seagrass complex similar to what once occurred in the area. The goal is to establish vegetation that can be sustainably, conserved, yet provide spawning and nursery grounds and aquaculture. Though still in its early stages, the prognosis is good. In fact Darwin, Australia recognized the value of its extensive mangrove swamps by establishing Charles Darwin National Park to protect them.

## 5.6 LESSONS FROM FERTILE, UNSTABLE HABITATS

Landslides, floodplains, lakeshores, mangroves and salt marshes represent a gradient of increasing substrate stability. Where fertile, landslides can rapidly develop plant cover but it can all disappear instantaneously in the next erosion event. Similarly, floodplains may develop tall forests in the fertile, moist sands and silts, but be denuded in a single flood. Lakeshores are less susceptible to erosion but flooding can drown established vegetation and lakes formed by dams can alternatively flood or desiccate their shores. Mangroves and salt marshes on low-energy seashores can be eroded or flooded, but the mangrove trees and salt marsh grasses help stabilize the substrate and can survive most natural disturbances. Stabilization is therefore the key to restoring all of these habitats, and human activities alter stability in various ways. Destabilization of slopes is aggravated by road building, logging or overgrazing. Stabilization of floodplains occurs from dams that prevent natural flood cycles and can allow weed invasions of native plant communities. Dams, drainage or other construction activities alter lake levels, while low-energy seashores can be damaged by in-filling and bulldozing for development. Restoration of these fertile, unstable sites requires humans to reduce their impacts and restore natural levels of stability.

BIBLIOGRAPHY

*Landslides*

Larsen, M. C. and Simon, A. (1993). A rainfall intensity-duration threshold for landslides in a humid–tropical environment, Puerto Rico. *Geografiska Annaler*, **75A**, 13–23.

Walker, L. R. and del Moral, R. (2003). *Primary Succession and Ecosystem Rehabilitation.* Cambridge: Cambridge University Press.

Walker, L. R., Zarin, D. J., Fetcher, N., Myster, R. W. and Johnson, A. H. (1996). Ecosystem development and plant succession on landslides in the Caribbean. *Biotropica*, **28**, 566–76.

Walker, L. R. and Willig, M. R. (1999). An introduction to terrestrial disturbances. In *Ecosystems of Disturbed Ground, Ecosystems of the World* 16, ed. L. R. Walker. Amsterdam: Elsevier, pp. 1–16.

## Floodplains

Ball, P. (2000). *Life's Matrix: a Biography of Water*. New York: Farrar, Straus and Giroux.

Hassan, F. A. (2005). A river runs through Egypt: Nile floods and civilization. *Geotimes*, **4**, 22−5.

Wohl, E. (2004). *Disconnected Rivers: Linking Rivers to Landscapes*. New Haven: Yale University Press.


## Lakeshores

Ferguson, R. (2003). *The Devil and the Disappearing Sea: A True Story About the Aral Sea Catastrophe*. Vancouver: Rain Coast Books.


## Mangroves

Hogarth, P. J. (2000). *Biology of Mangroves*. Oxford: Oxford University Press.

McKee, K. L., and Baldwin, A. H. (1999). Disturbance regimes in North American wetlands. In *Ecosystems of Disturbed Ground, Ecosystems of the World 16*, ed. L. R. Walker. Amsterdam: Elsevier, pp. 331−63.

United Nations (2006). *In the Front Line: Shoreline Protection and Other Ecosystem Services from Mangroves and Corals*. New York : United Nations Publishers.


## Estuaries

Dyer, K. R. (1998). *Estuaries: A Physiographic Introduction*. New York: John Wiley & Sons.

Haslett, S. K. (2001). *Coastal Systems*. New York: Routledge.

Packham, J. R. and Willis, A. J. (2001) *Ecology of Dunes, Salt Marsh and Shingle*. London: Chapman and Hall.

# 6

## Fertile and stable habitats

### 6.1 INTRODUCTION

Disturbances of fertile, stable habitats are often caused by natural events including fire, hurricanes, intense rainfall events and strong winds or by human activities that include intentionally set fires, agriculture, logging and grazing. Recovery following mild disturbances is normally rapid compared to intensely damaged sites because there is residual soil, vegetation and fauna and because the disturbance was not severe. However, wildfire, strong winds and human actions can lead to dramatic or subtle degradation of ecosystem properties on a site. When these more intense disturbances occur or chronic disturbances cease, the functioning of the system may have changed permanently and a return to productive ecosystems is not assured. The recovery then occurs in a new context, often quite different from that under which the ecosystem developed.

Today, many natural ecosystems across the world are in crisis. It is as if their immune systems have been compromised as combinations of natural and man-made disturbances become increasingly severe. How to manipulate the aftermath of these disturbances without loss of fertility or stability are lessons that silviculture and agriculture can learn from natural processes. Given that world agricultural production contributes about three quarters of global soil erosion, those lessons appear not yet to have been mastered.

How do ecosystems and humans respond to disturbances in stable habitats that cause relatively little loss of fertility? In these circumstances, disturbances may not cause much soil loss unless destabilized slopes are affected, so the nutrients are retained within the system, while plants and animals recycle them into new growth. Secondary succession describes how an ecosystem recovers from such damage, which is in contrast to most of our previous examples (volcanoes, glacial moraines, cliffs, floodplains), which exemplify primary succession.

Together, fires, hurricanes, torrential rain and domestic animal grazing produce overwhelming depletion in the croplands and pastures of this planet. In the twenty-first century, the same forces that once caused annoying damage now often trigger changes that overwhelm vegetation in fertile sites and limit their resilience. Ecosystems cannot repair themselves with sufficient speed after catastrophic fires, devastating wind and overgrazing to avoid large, negative impacts on humans. Humans must intervene to hasten the restoration of habitats damaged by these forces. Below we discuss how our understanding of succession can provide guidelines for the repair of systems damaged by fire, hurricanes and overgrazing.

## 6.2  FIRE

### 6.2.1  Introduction

Ecological studies of fire behavior, regimes and the biological impacts of fire provide several lessons for mitigating disasters. Natural fires (wildfires) are caused in most cases by lightning strikes, and these can be surprisingly frequent in tropical areas. Wildfires can rejuvenate the landscape and controlled burning is used throughout the world. Fires remove dead wood and litter, reduce soil-borne diseases and promote nutrient recycling. The heat of fire stimulates seed germination and removes growth inhibitors from the soil, while dormant buds in stems are also stimulated to burst into activity. This lush growth often promotes wildlife; for example, the Aboriginal inhabitants of Australia used fire to attract game that fed on the fresh grass growth. Many plant species are freed from competition, so biodiversity spikes with a bloom after a fire. Then many species subside to await the next fire. There is little long-term loss of fertility under normal conditions. Humans have always altered natural fire regimes, usually for practical reasons, such as land clearing for agriculture or to improve hunting. These intentional fires were usually controlled and often achieved the desired goals. However, extended fire suppression has changed the equation.

Fire suppression in the USA, Western Europe and elsewhere during the last eight decades has been based on the faulty notion that fire is solely a destructive force. Suppression could only be beneficial because the vegetation structure would be preserved, wildlife would thrive and the forest would achieve optimal functioning. This is the

---

**Box 6.1  Wildfires often overwhelm any response**

The Canberra (capital of Australia) bushfires of January 18, 2003 were the worst in its history and destroyed over 500 homes, damaged much of the infrastructure, nearly destroyed a major telescope facility and devastated a world-renowned nature preserve. The trauma remains evident in the human population with many opting to move elsewhere. Relatively few have rebuilt their homes. A long drought set the stage and lightning provided the spark. A firestorm of unprecedented fury attacked the suburbs after several days' burning many square kilometres of forest in the surroundings (Plate 13). Fireballs, hurled several kilometers from the leading edge of the flames, landed randomly among homes, scorching some, obliterating others and leaving some unscathed. Within a few hours, four people died and more than 500 homes were destroyed (Fig. 6.2). These effects occurred in a region that is extremely fire conscious and in suburbs where all prudent fire safety strategies were in place. This intense set of fires has caused fire ecologists to reevaluate models that describe how fires develop and explode.

---

"Smoky the Bear" syndrome, and while no one wants to see Smoky or Bambi burn, suppression has instead caused the return interval between fires to become unnaturally long. When fires ultimately reoccur, the accumulated fuels permit catastrophic firestorms that may destroy homes and take lives (Box 6.1). Wildlife suffers because it is impossible to outrun or to hide from such intense, rapidly moving fires. Rather than rejuvenation, the aftermath of high intensity fires includes floods, mudslides, severe erosion and limited ecosystem recovery. In the end, fire suppression policies have caused enormous economic losses and lowered ecosystem diversity and productivity. Many ecosystems become ripe for the invasion of exotic species in barren sites, while nutrient losses preclude rapid recovery.

Because humans have colonized many environments that had been historically fire prone, the management and control of fire is critical. Expensive homes dot the flammable hillsides from Barcelona (Fig. 6.1) to Santa Monica and from Cape Town to Adelaide. Unfortunately, fire management is fraught with thorny technical and social problems. To date there have been few studies on how to restore burned lands and reduce collateral damage. Where forestry prevails, the focus has been to replant commercially valuable species and the plantations

Fig. 6.1 Maquis near Barcelona (Spain). Fire-tolerant scrub vegetation such as this occurs in temperate summer-dry climates in Australia, South Africa, southern Chile, California and the Mediterranean basin.

are often monocultures. Near expanding cities, the focus has been to engineer prevention of future fires damaging structures. We know of no situation where vegetation management has successfully produced viable environments that effectively retard bush-fires, so building within fire-adapted vegetation remains hazardous.

Unintentional fires can be controlled to some extent and their impacts minimized. Lightning causes most fires, but occasionally devastating wildfires result from bizarre events. In 1965, a snake that had been dropped onto power lines by a hawk caused a 250,000 ha fire in Southern California chaparral. Recently, a large fire in Colorado (USA) resulted when a campfire that was started to burn love letters from an estranged lover, escaped control.

Intentionally set fires are often beneficial. Prescribed burns are one kind of intentional fire, lit by land managers following detailed protocols. These fires are often intended to improve vegetation vigor by facilitating nutrient cycling, thinning understories or removing litter to reduce fuel loads. Other purposes, sometimes at odds with the previous ones, include improving the vigor of wildlife and controlling invasive species such as undesirable shrubs in grasslands. Finally, some fires are used to convert forest or brush lands into pastures, or to clear land for agriculture.

Often, in the aftermath of fire, little needs to be done because natural processes will repair the damage. However, increasingly there should be a concerted response to mend the damage caused by fire. We explore in Section 6.2.5 how the adverse effects of fire can be ameliorated using succession principles.

### 6.2.2   Physical setting

Wildfires need fuel and do the most damage after extended periods of fuel build-up and long droughts. Mild winters, scant rainfall and prolonged, dry summers define the Mediterranean climate that is also found in the southwestern USA, South Africa, southern Australia and central Chile. The mild conditions foster dense vegetation and prolonged summer droughts provide desiccation to promote hot fires. Hot, dry winds such as the Santa Ana winds of southern California or the sirocco that emerges from Africa propel blazes with astonishing speed. The vegetation itself is replete with aromatic oils that enhance its flammability. As plants die, they are transformed into fuel, and litter builds up from the death of leaves because decomposition is slow. Rugged terrain provides further impetus because fires rapidly move up slopes, generating their own wind that can be further accelerated when funneled through canyons. Firestorms rival pyroclastic flows in generating terror as they rage unchecked across the land. The Mediterranean climates also experience thunderstorms, which are responsible for about 10 percent of wild fires. Most other fires result from human actions, usually accidental, but in North America, at least 25 percent result from arson. Fire frequency has increased in the last several decades because humans increasingly dwell in fire-prone forests.

Fires also occur in tropical forests. Small-scale fires were common for centuries, but recent large fires have occurred in such places as Brazil and Indonesia. In the Brazilian Amazon forests, fire is used to clear logging residuals, to control weeds, to create pastures or to harvest crops like sugar cane. These purposeful fires are sufficiently damaging to the natural forests, but they often escape to devastate the semi-deciduous forest.

In vegetation of colder climates such as taiga (a word that once referred to marshy Siberian forests, but now to any boreal forest), slow growing trees succumb to infrequent, but devastating fires, over 80 percent of which are of human origin (Box 6.2). Taiga comprises over 25 percent of the world's forest and covers 11 percent of the Northern

Box 6.2  **Fires in cold, wet habitats**

Forest fires in the Russian taiga threaten biodiversity and the global carbon balance. In addition to species common in cold forests, many southern species occur as relicts of warmer times. Unfortunately, the Russian fire management system is in shambles. Never efficient, it permits fires that exceed the threshold of recovery. While fire suppression in North America and western European boreal forests appears to promote local extinction of fire-adapted species, the increase of fire in Russia (80 to 90 percent caused by careless humans) is having a similar effect. The reduction of adverse effects of fire in Russia is a huge challenge that is being frustrated by lack of fire fighting capability, poor data and the general belief that the annual conflagrations that dominate the media each summer are just Nature's way. While lightning-caused fires have been part of the boreal ecosystem for millennia, the current situation of very frequent, extensive and intensive fires is a major detriment to the stability and diversity of the system.

Hemisphere. The Siberian taiga is the largest forest in the world, almost 6,000 km wide and 1,000 km from north to south. Huge quantities of carbon are fed into the atmosphere by taiga fires each year. With the arrival of Europeans in North America, wildfires became rampant. Over 75 percent of the spruce forests in Alaska have burned recently, and most regions in Canada have suffered fires. The $CO_2$ released contributes substantially to global warming. As previously frozen soils (permafrost) are exposed to sunlight, they thaw and release further $CO_2$, fueling what many fear is a runaway greenhouse effect.

### 6.2.3   Fire in the lives of humans

Most groups of humans have used fire as a tool, first for hunting, later to clear land for agriculture. Archeological evidence suggests that fire has been a hunting tool for thousands of years. Native Americans used fire to improve the prospects for hunting by clearing obstructing trees and increasing forage for their prey. In the Amazon, fire was used to open up forests and to improve soils for an agriculture that we have only recently realized existed. Historical mention of fire as a tool occurred well before Homer.

A recent study by Gifford Miller and his colleagues found evidence of a dramatic shift in the vegetation of central Australia about

50,000 years ago. Before then, there was little evidence of widespread fires. Trees and shrubs, with palatable grasses, dominated the vegetation. Aboriginal people then appeared, and the evidence suggests that fire frequency increased, most likely set by Aboriginals to improve hunting. However, the new fire regime appears to have altered the vegetation. The climatic evidence indicates that the Australian monsoon, which was weak between 40,000 and 60,000 years ago, did not recover, unlike the Indian monsoon. It is possible that the reduction in vegetation biomass started a feedback loop in central Australia that led to the failure of the monsoon to return. Shortly thereafter, most large, specialized herbivore marsupials that could not cope with vegetation dominated by less palatable grasses and desert shrubs became extinct. The hypothesis is that these extinctions were not due to hunting, but rather to inadvertent changes in vegetation due to an alteration in the disturbance regime and subsequent climate change.

Much of the tropics today can support humans only through the practice known as shifting agriculture. First a small patch of forest is cut and burned. The ash enriches the soil and a variety of crops can be grown for several years. When the soil loses fertility, the field is allowed to revert to forest and the process is repeated in another field. Typically, in Central America, the sequential use of several fields, each less than 0.5 ha in size, could support a family. With population growth and shifts to cash economies, slash-and-burn agriculture replaced shifting agriculture. Forests are now cleared as with shifting agriculture, but as harvests decline, the fields are converted to pastures rather than allowed to revert to forest. Once burned, a patch of land is given no chance to recover. Within the last few decades fire, once a valid agricultural tool, has become a weapon to destroy forests. The effect is particularly grave in tropical soils that are ancient and therefore extremely leached of nutrients. Extreme yellow soils (called podzols) in places like Borneo and northern Australia are virtually devoid of nutrients. The store of nutrients is in the living plants, so when the forest burns, the ecosystem collapses and regeneration is a very long-term process.

At the other extreme from tropical subsistence farmers are the affluent suburbanites who continue to build in fire-prone environments to enjoy a certain communion with nature. Notable examples are found in the foothills surrounding many cities in Mediterranean climates where fire prevention inevitably leads to a buildup of flammable materials and eventual conflagrations. A firestorm near San Francisco,

California (USA) in 1991 killed 25 people and destroyed 3,000 homes, and the Cedar Fire near Los Angeles, California (USA) destroyed nearly 4,000 homes and burned 3,000 km². The inevitable aftermath is a denuded landscape, floods and potentially lethal mudslides.

### 6.2.4   Ecological responses to fire

Natural vegetation is attuned to its disturbance regime, and fire is a good example. Fires vary in their size, intensity (heat), severity (damage), duration (fast or slow burning) and return interval (frequency). Each of these traits affects how the biota will respond. Variations in these traits permit different patterns of survivorship. Fire frequencies in woodlands and forests across the globe range from rare (as in the coastal forests of the Pacific Northwest, USA and in deserts) to both frequent and intense fires common in chaparral vegetation. Should a fire occur in vegetation that rarely experiences it, the consequences are devastating. When fire occurs after too long an interval, the accumulated fuel can severely disrupt the ecosystem. Thus, as discussed above, fire prevention, ironically, leads to devastating fires, followed by catastrophic erosion and floods.

The effects of most fires will also vary spatially as a function of the interactions between weather and fuel. This leads to a patchwork of vegetation that combines to display remarkable stability. Colonization of large burned patches will be more subject to chance than small ones because they are more isolated from surviving organisms. For this reason, recovery is slower in extensive burns.

In forests with natural fire regimes, ground fires rejuvenate the understory without killing most of the trees. Charcoal enriches the soil and fire stimulates seeds of trees like lodge pole pine to germinate. Other species grow best where fires have opened up the canopy (e.g. Sequoia and Douglas fir). Natural fires also remove dead wood and reduce fuel loads. Such fires are normally frequent and not severe. Organic matter is returned to the soil, ground level heterogeneity is increased and biodiversity is enhanced.

Fires are a selective disturbance. Fires can reduce the potential for outbreaks of damaging insects or fungal pathogens that are supported by decomposing wood or litter. A given fire may kill only some species, some growth-forms or some age classes. Because fires often create serendipitous results, they enhance heterogeneity. The characteristics of any particular fire also change as it progresses. Slow moving, long-burning fires can destroy organic matter in the soil because their heat penetrates to a greater depth than that of faster fires. Loss of organic matter reduces fertility and the heat kills seeds to a greater depth. Peat fires in northern environments are frequently very slow burning and can generate heat to greater depths, as the fuel sometimes burns underground. The chaparral vegetation of Southern California demonstrates how the species comprising the vegetation have evolved in response to repeated fires. That the vegetation in each of the Mediterranean climate regions of the world has similar traits even though their floras have little in common suggests the power of the selective force of fires. Each region also has many *pyrogenic* taxa. The oils of eucalyptus, pines and many aromatic species may reduce herbivory, but they certainly intensify fires.

Some species of large woody plants can survive fires. Thick bark may insulate living tissue so that leaves sprout from the charred stems (e.g. larches, redwoods, oaks and eucalyptus). More commonly, the shoots are killed, but underground parts called ligno-tubers sprout with the first rains. "Stump sprouters" such as manzanita and chamise in Southern California get a jump-start in reclaiming dominance. Other species, such as ceanothus, regenerate from a large bank of seeds that germinate with the first rains and can establish dense stands. The heat and smoke of the fire stimulates the seeds of a seed bank to germinate, so that a post-fire bloom is common. During this time, most chaparral species reproduce to create the next generation. The seeds stay dormant in the soil until the next fire. Species with bulbs can also remain dormant for decades.

Traits such as those described for chaparral vegetation interact with changing fire regimes that are due to fire prevention efforts, so subsequent recovery may differ from the long-term cycle. For example, fire suppression stretches the interval between fires, during which time the seed bank of some species may become exhausted and short-lived (*c.* 40 years) shrubs may die out. Alternatively, short intervals may exclude long-lived shrubs that have delayed reproduction or species with a short-lived seed bank. Within a given region, it is possible to determine the effects of altering fire regimes on the subsequent vegetation structure by taking the "vital attributes" of each species into account. Vital attributes include length of time to seed production, survival strategies and methods for regeneration, and so determine whether a species can regenerate during the fire interval and survive fires of different intensities.

When humans suppress fire and alter the fire regime, patterns change. The forest system becomes less resilient for several reasons.

Logging has exposed forests to disease, weeds and wind storms, increased erosion (through road building and soil disruption) and exhausted fertility. Fire suppression sometimes leads to disease outbreaks because dead or dying wood is a common host to pathogens. The inevitable fire produces raging firestorms that devastate vast areas and burn soil organic matter. The destruction from this type of fire is compounded in the aftermath when rain saturates the soil resulting in mudslides.

### 6.2.5   Human responses

In contrast to efforts described elsewhere, the human response to wildfires need not, nor does it usually, involve reintroduction of lost species. At most, fires severely damage the biota, but residual species and those readily able to colonize provide the biotic framework for the restoration of both structure and function of the vegetation. The human responses to fire fall into two broad categories. The first aims to reduce the economic and environmental costs of fires that can occur by pre-fire management and prevention. The second strives to mitigate the adverse effects resulting from fires.

*Traditional fire management*

The human response to wildfire has become increasingly proactive. Significant resources are expended to burn forests and brush in mild weather before it can burn under adverse conditions. In North America, most public and private forests used to be managed under a policy of complete fire control. Ironically, though this practice often successfully suppressed fires for decades, it produced a continent full of forests ready for conflagration – events that now happen regularly. Though the publicity campaign to categorize all forest fires as harmful has been moderated, "Smoky the Bear" remains the prime symbol for fire prevention. While this can be justified because humans cause 90 percent of forest and brush fires, it is hard to find information concerning the beneficial aspects of natural fires.

At the same time, population growth and affluence have prompted many to move into the hills. Today, prescribed burns are not feasible where so many homes are located and they are not advisable where so much fuel has accumulated, and we find that fire fighters, insurance companies and architects now cooperate to promote ways to mitigate damage. There are several strategies to reduce environmental and economic losses from future fires. Culturally important forests, such as those in Yosemite National Park, are managed by hand clearing of underbrush and saplings of undesirable tree species. Though expensive, this tactic appears to be successful in maintaining forests dominated by very large trees incapable of regenerating in a competitive regime. The structure of such forests will permit ground fires but resist the development of devastating crown fires because the distance from ground to first branches is large.

The policy of the US Forest Service and comparable organizations in other countries has evolved from total suppression to more nuanced responses. Fires that pose little threat are monitored, but permitted to run their natural course. Environmental conditions, vegetation characteristics and fire patterns can be evaluated in real time and conditions that would activate fire control measures are prepared in advance.

Healthy vegetation in fire climates exists in a mosaic of patches that differ in structure, age and species composition, but also reflect an underlying variation in fire intervals. Landscape mosaics created by management will reduce the extent of major fires. Matrices of different burn potentials may reduce the dangers of living in fire-prone habitats, but burned habitats need to be revegetated to prevent flooding and erosion.

### Living with fire potential

Like earthquakes and hurricanes, fires will happen. Just as one can retrofit a home against violent earth movements, or reduce hurricane damage by boarding up windows and cutting down nearby trees, homes can be made ready to resist wildfire. But no degree of preparation and planning can prevent a devastating result if the fire conditions are extreme (Fig. 6.2; Plate 13). The main precautions now focus on better fuel management and improving the awareness and understanding of residents about wildfires and what precautions to take during an emergency. Several approaches to preparing dwellings for intense fires have become prevalent in many regions, though even these preparations may prove insufficient against intense fires. Most homes now built near fire-prone vegetation are constructed of fire-resistant materials such as bricks, tile roofs, and metal shutters. The immediate surroundings are cleared of combustible materials, and trees within close proximity (30 m) should be thinned to reduce

Fig. 6.2 Bush fires can wreak terrible havoc (Canberra, Australia).
(a). Raging bush fires devastated the landscape: vegetation suffered a high
degree of mortality and soil erosion was common, but plants began to
recover once the winter rains began. (b). The smoldering remains of one
hard-hit suburb ravaged in a 2003 fire. Neither the city nor the countryside
has yet recovered. (Both images courtesy of David Mackenzie.)

the chance that fire will leap from forest to home. The ground layer
should be thinned and trees limbed to prevent ground fires from
reaching crowns. Fire risks to dwellings can be reduced, but no amount
of fireproofing will stop the worst fires, and some jurisdictions in

---

**Box 6.3 The legacy of the Yellowstone fires**

Studies of post-fire recovery of ecosystems at Yellowstone National Park in 1988 continue to provide many ecological lessons, some of them offering many surprises. Even though this landscape was devastated by an intense wildfire following decades of fire suppression, there was a significant residual biota ready to sprout, and native ground cover responded quickly (Fig. 6.3). Therefore little rehabilitation was required. The fires did not reduce landscape variation. The post-fire landscape was a mosaic of unburned and burned sites, with the latter having experienced fires of different severity. Most burned sites were close to unburned sites, ensuring that dispersal would compensate for species losses. Coarse woody debris left in the aftermath has proven invaluable to the regeneration of the ecosystem. Standing dead trees (snags) attract birds, and so aid dispersal of species with fleshy fruits. Downed logs offer protection to small animals and to establishing seedlings, while decomposing debris adds organic matter to the soil. These large fires were part of a millennial-scale process of stand rejuvenation. Though infrequent, small fires occurred in this region with sufficient frequency to prevent catastrophic fires. Where fire suppression has been practiced, fuel loads have shifted the fire regime from understory burns to conflagrations. Natural crown fires create important landscape heterogeneity, with stands of different ages and different biotic complements. This spatial variation is crucial to the health of such ecosystems. The Yellowstone study clearly demonstrates that interventions are not always required to facilitate vegetation recovery.

---

severely fire-prone environments have recognized this and have simply banned further development.

The use of fire-resistant vegetation in firebreaks was proposed as a tactic to control fires, but this promise has not been realized. While the vegetation may burn more slowly, it still burns, and firebreaks are often jumped during the windy conditions that fan many fires. In South Africa, natural vegetation was a quite effective firebreak, but for decades the trees of this vegetation have been cut for their valuable timber in a resource-poor environment.

Long-term strategies to reduce fire intensity involve different economic management tactics. Selectively cutting smaller, yet

Fig. 6.3 Yellowstone National Park vegetation mosaic (Wyoming, USA). The great 1988 conflagration left behind a patchwork of vegetation burned to different degrees. Surviving remnants and buried seeds provided the means for relatively rapid vegetation recovery.

commercially valuable trees produces more open forests in which meadows can be interspersed with trees. Meadow vegetation is less prone to fire than are dense understories of shrubs, so this type of vegetation reduces fire intensity and the ability of fires to carry through the forest. Reduced density of faster growing trees also limits the spread of diseases.

### Dealing with the aftermath

To the degree that planning and pre-burn mitigation efforts work, then erosion and mudslides will be reduced. Nevertheless, fires do occur and if they have devastated the landscape, restoration must be considered.

Studies of the recovery of ecosystems after fire (e.g. in Yellowstone; Fig. 6.3; Box 6.3) have provided many ecological lessons that can be applied to recovering from the damage from intense fires. There is a significant residual biota ready to sprout with the first rains after even the most intense fire. However, in steep terrain, these rains often cause landslides and floods because vegetation has not recovered. Irrigating strips of land before natural rains to stimulate early germination and growth may sometimes work. In very large disturbances, key species may require introduction.

Nitrogen and other nutrients are frequently lost and, if rapid regeneration is needed in commercial forests, fertility needs to be restored. Light fertilization early in the first growing season will promote recovery and reduce erosion. Because hot fires destroy seed banks, clearing of fuel and prescribed burning can be used to reduce the intensity of fires and promote biodiversity. In some critical areas, erosion has to be controlled by mechanical means until vegetation can recover.

### 6.2.6   Links with other disturbances

The mismanagement of fire creates a cascading effect of devastation. What is worse, some computer models suggest that more of the planet will become increasingly susceptible to intense fires as global warming develops. The expansion of drought-afflicted vegetation will increase fire frequencies, increase the level of $CO_2$ in the atmosphere and possibly accelerate the rate of global warming. So there will be a potentially vicious feedback cycle leading to more fires, more carbon in the air, higher temperatures, greater drought and, finally, still more fires.

Though grazing can reduce the susceptibility to fire, it also limits the ability of a system to recover fully following a fire. As a result, productivity and economic value may be degraded. Fires and livestock grazing combine to denude hillsides and lead to landslides and mudflows. Generally, it is inadvisable to graze during the season following a fire. Major landslides and mudflows are common where fire suppression eventually leads to conflagrations. Subsequent deluges quickly saturate the landscape. Where the land has been cleared by fire on steep slopes, mountains are denuded. Hurricane Mitch in 1998 inundated much of Central America, arguably the most devastating environmental disaster in its recent history. While Hurricane Mitch was the agent of an unprecedented disaster, fire set the stage, and erosion was made worse by logging roads. A century of habitat conversion facilitated by fires converted forest to patchworks of small fields and bare soil, and then torrential rains simply swept the soil away.

Recurrent fires, common in anthropogenic landscapes, can lead to conversion of vegetation from, for example, woodland to scrub steppe.

These conversions are more common in semi-arid and Mediterranean climates. Fires are linked directly to many other aspects of environmental degradation. Making effective responses to the challenges posed by more intense, frequent fires will test our abilities to cope with chronic problems. Learning how to manage fire and to reduce the impacts of intense fires will repay the effort manyfold.

## 6.3 HURRICANES

### 6.3.1 Introduction

There is no such thing as a benign hurricane. These powerful windstorms, named for the Arawak storm god Hanaka, have the capacity to destroy lives and property. They can have the force of 20 nuclear explosions per hour. Even over remote oceans, hurricanes can severely damage coral reefs. Coastal residents rightly worry about seasonal monsters that may become more destructive as global warming leads to warmer oceans. But such worries have not slowed the dash to build beach homes and exclusive tourist facilities throughout the tropical hurricane belt. Coastal residents increased by 75 percent in Florida, USA between 1980 and 2003. By 2025, half of the world's population will live where they are at risk from hurricanes. Consequently, estimates of property damage increase every year.

How do people cope with such unpredictable hazards as hurricanes? How do plants, animals and people recover from the damage? Are there lessons to be learned from natural recovery processes that will aid human responses to these disturbances? In addition to the obvious direct damage that hurricanes cause, indirect damage may have long-term effects (e.g. destruction of mangroves and dunes, salt water intrusion into aquifers, silt damage to coral reefs). Learning the limits and patterns of destruction and ecological recovery helps humans avoid vulnerable areas, minimize damage with proper building codes, avoid loss of human lives with evacuation plans and adopt the most efficient restoration efforts.

### 6.3.2 Physical setting

Global wind patterns are established by differential heating of the earth's surface and by the earth's spin that create massive circulation systems called Hadley cells. The tropics (between 23.5° N or S of the Equator) receive the most direct sunlight and therefore receive the most energy on earth. Heated air rises, cools, loses some moisture as rain and then spreads toward the poles. Where cool winds descend and warm, there is drought, as illustrated by the many deserts between 20–40° N and S.

Hurricanes (also called typhoons or cyclones) are storms with sustained winds of more than 118 km/h that are generated by warm, moist air rising from tropical waters. Hurricanes are most common in tropical and subtropical regions where ocean waters are sufficiently warm. However, with increasing frequency, they continue from their tropical origins into temperate zones in Japan, southern Australia or northeastern North America. Hurricanes have devastating, spiraling winds. In the center, or eye, of the spiral the winds are calm. Some windstorms do not meet the hurricanes criteria yet they still cause disasters. In October 1987, for example, a windstorm devastated Great Britain with winds more than 176 km/h, reducing old forests to tumbled wrecks. The worst storm in the UK since 1703, it flattened 15 million trees and left 19 people dead. Typically, hurricane winds weaken rapidly once over land and away from their source of heated water. However, if they return to the ocean, they can regain their force.

### 6.3.3 Hurricanes in the lives of humans

Predictable winds have long served humans for exploration, trade and the generation of power. The Polynesians explored the islands in the Pacific Ocean from 1500 BC to AD 1000. The Chinese and Mongols dominated the oceans throughout Asia until AD 1500. European sailing ships (c. AD 1500 to 1900) used the trade winds to reach America and rode the winds of the Gulf Stream back home. Today, jet streams reduce trans-Atlantic travel time for eastbound airplanes by about one hour. Early windmills ground flour, pumped water and drained fens and polders. Modern wind turbines generate electricity. They are an increasing feature of landscapes on windy ridges from Brazil to Inner Mongolia and are even found in shallow seas off the coast of Denmark.

We cannot predict the number or timing of windstorms in more than a general way. Some recent evidence suggests that the number of hurricanes in the Atlantic each year is positively correlated with a weak El Niño in the Pacific and storms over West Africa. Predictions about the exact paths hurricanes will take, even if only hours in advance, are also improving. Daredevil pilots have measured wind currents that steer hurricanes by flying both around the outside of the storm and into the center, or eye, of the hurricane. Such measurements have increased predictability of hurricane trajectories two to three days in advance. Another recent discovery may further aid the tracking of hurricanes. Hurricanes apparently draw ozone down from as high as 16 km in the atmosphere, creating an ozone concentration near ground level at their centers, but ozone depletion in the spinning air. By monitoring ozone levels, scientists might better track future hurricanes. The most difficult aspect of a hurricane to predict is its intensity, typically measured by wind speed (see above). Because intensity determines the amount of damage likely to result, there is much interest in improving this area of hurricane prediction.

Has global warming increased hurricane frequency? Some are concerned that the demonstrated increase in tropical ocean temperatures of about 0.6 °C since 1970 will mean greater hurricane frequency. The jury is still out on this question. There is large, decade-long variation in the number of hurricanes within a given area such as the Atlantic and we are currently undergoing a period of relatively high hurricane frequency. More variation occurs when one compares hurricane frequencies around the world. With only several decades of good records, it is too early to say if the global rise in tropical oceanic waters will lead to increased hurricane frequency. However, there is a consensus that hurricane intensity (as measured by wind speed) and rainfall have both increased due to more evaporation from warmer oceans. One prediction suggests that by 2080 global warming could cause the typical hurricane to produce 6 percent stronger winds and 18 percent more rain.

Property damage by hurricanes is related to wind speed, duration of the storm, building densities and building values. It is also affected by the degree of natural protection afforded by the coast. Marshes, dunes and reefs can absorb the impact of hurricanes to lessen inland damage. However, property damage is inevitable as long as people build in hurricane zones. An increasing portion of the population has no choice. Many hurricanes have resulted in large numbers of fatalities, often from secondary causes such as flooding. Hurricane Katrina (2005), the most expensive storm for the USA, also resulted in over 1,600 deaths. The most deadly hurricane ever recorded was in Bangladesh in 1970. At least 300,000 people were killed by storm surges in that low-lying country (Table 1.1). Improvement in predictability would certainly save lives, as long as residents are able to respond to emergency evacuations.

Fig. 6.4 Rainforests of the Caribbean National Forest (Puerto Rico) before Hurricane Hugo. The intact rainforest demonstrates strong root buttresses, large palms and epiphytes.

### 6.3.4    Ecological responses to hurricanes

How does a tropical or sub-tropical forest recover following a hurricane? To answer this question we first need to know how much damage occurred. It is ideal when detailed descriptions of the vegetation before the hurricane are available (Fig. 6.4). Did most trees lose their leaves but remain standing? Perhaps only smaller branches were broken? How was the pattern distributed on the landscape (Fig. 6.5)? What percentage of trees had their trunks snapped (Plate 14; Fig. 6.6)? Were trees uprooted to create habitat heterogeneity and susceptibility to erosion (Fig. 6.7; Fig. 6.8)? Once damage is assessed, we can evaluate recovery. Can the dominant plants recover by sprouting from the branches, trunks or roots? To the degree this occurs, the forest gap will largely fill in from growth of existing trees. However, changes in plant species composition will occur if a different set of species fills the gap. Species change happens when the new species germinate from seeds (following either

Fig. 6.5  Aerial view of damage done by the powerful Hurricane Hugo (Puerto Rico). Even though this Force 5 hurricane devastated much of the Caribbean and the southeastern coast of the USA, patches of trees survived. (Courtesy of Ariel E. Lugo.)

dispersal into the gap or survival in the soil) or grow from pre-existing but suppressed seedlings in the understory. Often, several groups of plants dominate the gap regrowth in sequence.

There are many factors that determine the direction of forest succession after a hurricane, making the process and endpoint about as unpredictable as the original trajectory of the hurricane! In addition to which plants survive, arrive, grow, and compete most successfully, the timing of the disturbance is critical, relative to the growth and reproductive stages of likely colonizing plants. If the creation of a gap is followed by massive seed production of a particular species, that species may dominate the regeneration process. Likewise, the local climate following the hurricane is important. After Hurricane Hugo struck Puerto Rico in September 1989 (Box 6.4), loss of forest leaves prompted a three-month drought in the understory. Forest recovery was greatly retarded by that drought.

Animals, both aboveground and in the soil, also have character-istic responses to a hurricane. Birds may lose nesting sites but can often

Fig. 6.6  Cyclone Monica caused extensive forest damage (Jabiru, Northern Territory, Australia, 2006). The trunks of trees snapped if they were firmly rooted.

fly out of the danger zone, then return as food resources reappear. Some animal populations decline and rarely or slowly recover (e.g. some herbivorous insects). Others recover quickly following an initial decline (e.g. insectivorous bats that feed on new populations of leaf litter-based insects). Finally, other animal populations can influence plant growth and forest succession. Again, timing of the disturbance, overlaid by the life stages of the dominant animals, can influence recovery.

### 6.3.5  Human responses

First priorities following hurricanes usually include reestablishment of disrupted services such as water, gas and electricity and attention to removal of debris and reconstruction of damaged buildings. However, whether supervised or not, plants and animals eventually recover and recolonize the disturbed area. As noted above, the most obvious lessons on how to direct or accelerate such regrowth come from traditional shifting agriculture. When human population densities were lower than they are today, and each farmer would not revisit a short-term agricultural plot for several decades, this method of farming was

Fig. 6.7 Hurricane Hugo destroyed forests and initiated erosion throughout the Caribbean in 1989. This large root ball was among the many exposed by that storm. Species such as *Cecropia* colonized exposed soil where competition for light was reduced, but erosion was accelerated.

sustainable. Modern tropical farmers can sustain a longer cycle when they use a variety of crops with different maturation dates and variable structure (e.g. fast-growing annuals combined with slower-growing shrubs, trees and vines). These methods prolong the benefits of the gap and support denser human populations. They also mimic natural successional replacements, as some crops do well initially, while others produce at later stages. However, under modern economic pressures, it is more likely that the cycle is broken in favor of pastures for cattle and the expanded clearing of the rainforest.

### 6.3.6   Links with other disturbances

The high winds of hurricanes cause much direct damage, but flooding and erosion often cause indirect damage as well. Cyclone Larry (2006) destroyed many crops just ready for harvest in Queensland, Australia. Hurricane Katrina (2005) led to disastrous flooding of New Orleans,

Fig. 6.8 Cyclone Monica caused major damage to structures when trees were toppled (Jabiru, Northern Territory, Australia, 2006). Well-watered trees with shallow roots were particularly susceptible to uprooting.

---

**Box 6.4  Surviving the storm**

The first half of Hurricane Hugo (Puerto Rico, 1989) was intense. Lawrence cowered in his bathroom, the room with the smallest window, while other windows buckled and broke from the 200 kph winds. Venturing out during the passage of the eye of the storm he noticed that all but one of the purple-flowering crepe myrtle trees on his street had fallen down. The next day he drove among fallen trees and tilting telephone poles to the rainforest to assess the damage to ecological research facilities. Walking around toppled bamboo clumps, he and his colleagues eventually reached the nearly unscathed field station. However, after a harrowing hike, mostly four to five meters above the ground on fallen tree trunks, he discovered that a canopy research tower was a twisted wreck, resembling a pretzel, and was out of action. Researchers are still studying the impacts of Hurricane Hugo and subsequent storms on the recovery of the only tropical rain forest in the US National Forest system.

much of it exacerbated by a man-made shipping channel that funneled storm surges toward the levees. Hurricane Mitch (1998) destroyed mangroves and forests and caused massive landslides, floods and crop damage in Central America. Extensive fires burned the trees killed by Hurricane Gilbert in 1988 in Mexico. Such major loss of forests leads to a cascade of secondary effects including secondary succession, alterations in herbivore populations, and potentially drought from the reduction of evaporation and transpiration from tree leaves into the local atmosphere. Indeed, for three months following Hurricane Hugo in Puerto Rico (1989), the average elevation of cloud formation (dependent on moisture from the forests) rose from 500 to 900 m above sea level. Hurricanes can also trigger swarms of weak earthquakes, as first discovered with Hurricane Charley (Florida, August 2004). A sudden seismic spike as Charley moved back out to sea could have been from the storm triggering a sub-oceanic landslide. Hurricanes also damage coral reefs, so their damage is not limited to aboveground ecosystems. When the next hurricane hits, or a tsunami transpires, coastlines without the protection of reefs and mangroves are more susceptible to damage than those that retain intact coastlines.

Hurricanes are not isolated events. The land surface that is altered has a history that determines its present vegetation structure, topography and susceptibility to wind damage. This history reflects the combined effects of all disturbances that have struck this area. For example, in Puerto Rico, seedlings of *Cecropia* (a common tropical gap colonist) dominated regrowth on a landslide for several years until a hurricane knocked them down. This allowed tree ferns (*Cyathea*) to dominate regrowth for the next decade. Where *Cecropia* was not damaged, tree ferns did not dominate. Hurricanes are particularly dramatic examples of windstorms, and, like all windstorms, are part of a larger disturbance regime.

## 6.4   GRAZING

### 6.4.1   Overview

Grazing occurs naturally in most ecosystems (Fig. 6.9). In this case, the vegetation has evolved responses to its herbivores, and predators control herbivore numbers, so overgrazing is uncommon. However, unchecked grazing by exotic animals creates a litany of catastrophes, from the extinction of species to desertification (Box 6.5). Unfortunately, overgrazing is the rule throughout most human-dominated systems.

Fig. 6.9 Rocky Mountain goat in the Olympic National Park (Washington, USA). This species is common in subalpine forests of western North America where it rarely does lasting harm. However, in the Olympic Mountains, where goats were introduced for hunting, they threaten fragile vegetation and endemic species. Most have been removed by the Park Service to protect both the flora and the habitat.

---

**Box 6.5 Introduced mammals in New Zealand**

Before the colonization of New Zealand by humans, c. AD 1100, terrestrial mammals were non-existent there. Since Captain Cook's visit in 1770, exotic species have run rampant on both main islands. While the Australian possum is the most damaging exotic species, feral animals such as goats and deer have devastated forest landscapes. The contemporary vegetation has been drastically altered, with few surviving broad-leaved palatable species and dominance by unpalatable ones. Browsed forests are more open and less diverse than non-browsed forests. There are even less obvious effects on soil properties and litter ecosystems. The casual visitor to New Zealand is overwhelmed by the beauty, but is unaware of the transformations that have occurred in less than 200 years.

Today's landscapes in such different habitats as Greece, Utah (USA), Queensland (Australia), Xinjiang Province (China) and Morocco share one trait: they have been severely degraded by overgrazing from livestock. This impact is subtle, chronic and ubiquitous. Because it is tied to the well-being and economy of nearly all humans, grazing can cause far more environmental havoc than either fire or wind. In this section, we describe how overgrazing leads to disaster and how landscapes can be brought back from the brink of irreversible devastation.

### 6.4.2    Physical setting

Overgrazing has three main causes. The most frequent cause occurs where grazing lands are treated as commons. In commons, everyone has an equal stake in the land. Each individual derives all the benefits from his herd, while the damage done to the land is shared communally. Because the benefits are readily appreciated, while the damage is gradual, the degradation process continues. There are few regulations to limit the number of animals in a commons. Rangeland and pastures throughout the world have been, and in many places continue to be, devastated by overstocking. This is a huge factor in desertification. The often-romanticized American West of the nineteenth century is the classic case, and the process continues today. The American West was once lush with palatable forage, and no regulations limited the number of cattle. From the 1860s to the 1950s, more livestock were maintained than could possibly be sustained. The predictable result was a reduction in the ability of the land to sustain herbivores. This pattern has recurred wherever European herding methods were introduced to a flora lacking ungulate grazers. Australia and South America are the prime examples. In much of Africa, herbivores have increased, but for much more complex reasons.

A second cause of overgrazing is less common. Native populations of herbivores often experience population explosions when their predators are severely controlled. In North America, deer populations routinely explode to ruin their habitat when cougars or wolves are eliminated. They have overwhelmed many forests, destroyed vegetation, affected other wildlife and spread pestilence (e.g. Lyme disease). When wolves were driven to extinction in Yellowstone National Park, a population explosion of elk followed. Such cases often lead to dramatic declines in the vitality of the vegetation.

---

**Box 6.6  What sporting fun**

In 1859, Thomas Austin released 24 rabbits onto his estate near the Victorian town of Geelong (Australia). Within 30 years, Victoria and New South Wales were swarming with rabbits, and by 1900 they were ubiquitous in grazing land throughout the continent. Why did Mr. Austin do this? Rabbits, he explained, are fun to shoot.

The rabbit is Australia's worst animal pest, though, unlike the cane toad, it cannot kill you. Costs of control and production losses are staggering. Repairing environmental damage done by rabbits will be a monumental task. Rabbits threaten the extinction of plants, birds, marsupials and insects, including unique species such as wombats, quolls, bandicoots and many others. Warrens and the removal of grass and shrubs promote erosion and the invasion of exotic plants, and thwart reforestation efforts. Do not bring up the subject of rabbits with an Australian, whether he is a stockman (ten rabbits eat as much as one sheep) or an environmentalist (whole ecosystems are being destroyed). Your ears might get burnt from the colorful language.

---

The third type of overgrazing has less justification than the first two, which occur due to understandable processes. In many parts of the world, large mammals have been introduced for sport. These species, lacking natural predators, frequently undergo astonishing population explosions, to wreak havoc on natural vegetation (Box 6.6).

Overgrazing is most severe in poor and densely populated countries. As human numbers increase, the need to restore overgrazed, degraded land will increase, but merely reducing stocking numbers will be insufficient. Restoration will be required because many species will have been eliminated and the presence of too many animals for too long can profoundly alter soil processes, hydrological regimes and nutrient cycling. No solution will be possible without addressing the interactions between overgrazing and habitat degradation.

### 6.4.3   Grazing in the lives of humans

Overgrazing is most severe in semi-arid landscapes where plant growth is water limited. Here, even modest grazing can devastate the landscape. The margins of the Sahara in southern Africa, central Asia, much of inland Australia, interior South America, northern Mexico and much of western USA are areas where livestock overgraze the land. These habitats are susceptible to salinization, wind erosion and desertification, all of which intensify the effects of grazing.

Modern pastoralism is at the root of much overgrazing. Before colonization by Europeans, pastoralism in Africa worked well. The social structure had controls that minimized the potential for overuse. Colonial powers drew national boundaries with little regard for indigenous people, and mobility was restricted. With greater health care populations exploded, and money became more important than barter. The logic of the commons came into force. Combined with climate fluctuations and the breakdown of the traditional pastoral way of life, the logic of the commons has facilitated desertification. No longer is the system sustainable, and a spiral of degradation may only be arrested by major interventions. Restoration of degraded land is one form of intervention.

Overgrazing is a global catastrophe. Dust clouds from northwest China drift across the United States, sometimes obscuring the Rocky Mountains. This signals alarming erosion in western China where grazing lands are becoming desert. Each year topsoil in an area twice the size of Hong Kong blows away and much more is deteriorating. Yet seasonal storms in China are getting stronger and starting sooner each year, probably in response to higher temperatures. Dust, combined with urban pollutants, is causing international outcry. Water scarcities are increasing and many lakes have disappeared in just 30 years. The blowing sands created by overgrazing have caused farmers to abandon their farms because you cannot plant a crop on a sand dune.

The introduction of large vertebrates into virgin territory occasionally provides limited benefits that partially offset the long-term damage. One such case was the introduction of camels into Australia by 1840. They made it possible for the ill-fated Burke and Wills expedition to cross a searing desert from western Victoria to the Gulf of Carpentaria in 1860. The hapless explorers released the camels when they reached coastal swamps. Without camels, and with no wilderness survival skills, all but one of the members of the expedition perished on the return journey. Camels continued to be imported to Australia until 1907. Although they helped to open central Australia and build railroads, most were released to the wild when they were no longer useful. Today, up to a million run wild and cause significant overgrazing in desert Australia (Fig. 6.10). They reduce forage for livestock and marsupials alike, leading to strange anti-camel alliances between stockmen and conservationists. They damage native trees, particularly those around water holes. The existence of some rare marsupials and emus is

Fig. 6.10  A camel in the East MacDonnell Ranges, near Alice Springs (Northern Territory, Australia). Like feral goats, domesticated and feral camels have intensified desertification in arid parts of Africa and Central Asia as well as in Australia. (Courtesy of Elizabeth Powell.)

threatened by camels. At least camels still support tourism in the form of desert safaris and can be found at county fairs, giving rides.

### 6.4.4  Ecological responses

Grazing can affect vegetation at several stages. Minor grazing can stimulate vegetation growth by trimming senescent plant material. Vertebrate grazers return nutrients to the soil in their dung and, eventually, in their decaying bodies. They can also disperse seeds. Seedlings are prone to being consumed by small vertebrates and even minor browsing kills young plants. When grazing intensifies, successional trajectories are altered. Moderate grazing is selective, so those species that are not consumed will persist. Released from competition, these plants thrive. Often changes are subtle and variations in vegetation composition can be ascribed to chance. In reality, variation in vegetation may be due to variable grazing pressures. For example, exclusion of voles in a wetland restoration project led to very different vegetation from the anticipated target.

When grazing intensity exceeds plant productivity, a threshold leading to inevitable degradation is crossed. When the threshold is crossed due to grazing by exotic animals, the descending spiral is accelerated because the plant species have few mechanisms to deter grazing. Introduced herbivores have little to check their population growth. Unpalatable plant species increase at first while palatable ones decline to extinction. Exotic weed species invade and dominate the landscape, and biodiversity plummets.

Overgrazing by livestock and subsequent landscape degradation is widespread, but how can human populations stabilize this intrinsically unstable system? The answer lies in balancing resource extraction, such as grazing, with resource renewal, such as fertilization or fallow periods, or by reducing stocking densities. There is a maximum number of herbivores that any ecosystem can support without degradation. That maximum is called the carrying capacity. Any population that exceeds its carrying capacity will eventually decline or crash in numbers. This decline can be rapid, as when populations of introduced elk on Alaskan islands crashed from hundreds to just several animals when all their forage was eaten. Alternatively, the number of herbivores can reach a dynamic balance, fluctuating around the carrying capacity. This equilibrium has been the goal of pastoralists for millennia and range scientists for decades. Luckily, most ecosystems have some flexibility or lag around the carrying capacity, but if resources are depleted for too long, numbers will decline. Artificially high numbers of herbivores (or humans on this planet) can be sustained for a while with massive inputs of fertilizers (for livestock) or resource extraction (such as oil for human use). The higher numbers go, however, the more the risk that the population will crash rather than diminish gradually. Sometimes a new, lower carrying capacity is established following a population crash because so many resources are removed that the original population levels can no longer be sustained. Humans that depleted the forests on Easter Island are one example.

Overgrazing also impacts other species: Australian ground-foraging birds, amongst the most threatened in Australia, are in full retreat in the face of increasing livestock and weeds. In overgrazed woodlands, birds expend more energy to avoid prey and have fewer favorable sites to forage. Tree creepers, wagtails and robins are among the afflicted species in weedy pastures. Simply reducing or eliminating livestock will not restore these woodlands. Weed reduction and the active reestablishment of eucalyptus and other species used as food sources are needed.

---

**Box 6.7  One small victory for restoring a balance**

Goats (*Capra hircus*) are infamous for their ability to eat most
vegetation to the ground. They have established on many islands
where, inevitably, they become feral. Without predators, wily goats
degrade their habitat. As the standing vegetation declines, erosion
reduces productivity and soils dry out. The usual result is the loss of
biodiverity and the establishment of weeds. However, by combining
aerial hunting from helicopters with hunting dogs and Judas goats,
about 120 small islands around the world have had their goats
eradicated. These programs are in their early stages but it is hoped
they will be followed by plans for restoration of the vegetation.

---

### 6.4.5  Human responses to grazing

Overgrazing is global, but human numbers suggest that the problem
will never abate. However, there are signs of hope. Degradation due
to overgrazing can be reversed, but several steps are required for
restoration. We will confine our discussions to cases involving feral
domestic animals such as sheep and goats, the most common situation
in which vegetation restoration is possible, and to rangelands.

In sites to be restored, the offending animals should be removed,
at least temporarily (Box 6.7). Then degradation must be reversed by soil
rehabilitation, reintroduction of suitable vegetation or the addition of
nutrients. One example demonstrates how restoration can occur in
severely grazed landscapes.

In southwestern Australia, woodlands dominated by salmon gum
(*Eucalyptus salmonophloia*) occur in the fragmented landscapes of the
mixed farming 'wheat belt'. Cattle and sheep have overgrazed the
remnant woodlands, encouraging weeds to invade. After decades of
overgrazing, little of the former shrubby understory remains and
recruitment of salmon gum is close to zero. Restoration of saplings
and an understory is a difficult proposition, but began here with the
exclusion of stock and rabbits. Soil was "ripped" to alleviate compaction
and several plant species were introduced as large seedlings. The results
were mixed, but indicated that substantial intervention was required
for even modest success at reestablishing functioning woodlands.
Competition from adult salmon gums was a significant barrier to
restoration of its own seedlings, though other species profited. Soil
improvement was essential, and thinning the canopy improved overall
success.

In semi-arid South Africa, cattle have degraded large tracts and removed vegetation. Bare patches showed up clearly in satellite images. In order to prepare for revegetation, livestock were excluded. Restoration involved tilling to alleviate soil compaction, seeding pasture grasses and shrubs to hasten recolonization and layering with dead branches. Branches protected seedlings from drought and from herbivores until the plants were established. This approach proved to be both economical and effective.

Rangeland rehabilitation usually requires several difficult stages set in an appropriate social context. Grazing should be limited, fire is often introduced to limit exotic woody species and many other methods can be employed to limit weeds. When native species are reintroduced and fully established, some low levels of grazing may be permitted. However, the system will fail unless land management is integrated with the local system of ownership and law.

Overgrazing often leads to dominance by weeds and strong reductions in production that cut dramatically into standards of living. In the Andes, overgrazing reduced productivity by 60 percent because weeds dominated the pastures. Low productivity sites cannot be abandoned because even the limited productivity is essential for survival, and restoration under these conditions does not seem practical.

### 6.4.6   Links with other forms of disturbance

Overgrazing is linked to several processes. The closest links are to desertification and the formation of sand dunes in range areas. When grazing destabilizes vegetation, wind and water erosion increases. Dust clouds increase and agricultural productivity declines. In wetter situations, landslides become more common and lakes begin to fill more rapidly by siltation.

Grazing by domestic livestock on semi-natural lands interacts with many other forms of disturbance to accelerate the rate of degradation. In the deserts of southeastern California, overgrazing combines with the use of off-road vehicles, road construction, utility transmission corridors, military training and suburbanization to fragment and degrade fragile ecosystems. Several of these processes intensify the pervading air pollution that moves from large urban centers to the west. These soil disturbances have promoted exotic species and increased the frequency of fires, transforming native shrub communities to vegetation dominated by exotic annuals. These fragile systems have limited resilience, with estimates to a return of pre-disturbance levels of biomass and plant cover ranging from 50 to 300 years. Complete recovery, including biodiversity, could take at least ten times as long. It is clear that restoration is required to hasten recovery when sites are protected from disturbance.

### 6.5   LESSONS FROM FERTILE, STABLE HABITATS

When disturbances such as fire, hurricanes and grazing do not substantially lower site fertility or alter substrate stability, the course of recovery depends on the outcome of competition among those plants that either quickly disperse by seed into the site or that survive the disturbance. Growth can be rapid and often little or no intervention is needed. Severe fires or hurricanes and chronic grazing can, however, drastically reduce the ability of an area to recover because of secondary erosion of soil nutrients and organic matter as well as loss of seeds. Restoration can be much delayed and quite difficult if both soil and plants need reintroduction to the site. Undesirable weeds often dominate the early succession stages by successfully out-competing native plants. Humans depend on croplands and grasslands to sustain us, yet most soil erosion comes from agricultural lands. It is imperative that soil conservation be promoted through more ecologically aware land use and restoration activities.

BIBLIOGRAPHY

*Fire*

Bond, W. J. and van Wilgen, B. W. (1996). *Fire and Plants*. London: Chapman & Hall.
Bradstock, R. A., Bedward, M., Gill, A. M. and Cohn, J. S. (2005). Which mosaic? A landscape ecological approach for evaluating interactions between fire regimes, habitat and animals. *Wildlife Research*, **32**, 409–23.
Chase, A. (1987). *Playing God in Yellowstone*. New York: Harcourt Brace.
Grove, A. T. and Rachham, O. (2001). *The Nature of Mediterranean Europe: An Ecological History*. New Haven, CT: Yale University Press.
Keeley, J. E., Fotheringham, C. J. and Baer-Keeley, M. (2005). Determinants of post-fire recovery and succession in Mediterranean-climate shrublands of California. *Ecological Applications*, **15**, 1515–34.
Noble, I. R. and Slatyer, R. O. (1980). The use of vital attributes to predict successional changes in plant-communities subject to recurrent disturbances. *Vegetatio*, **43**, 5–21.
Turner, M. G., Romme, W. H. and Tinker, D. B. (2003). Surprises and lessons from the 1988 Yellowstone fires. *Frontiers in Ecology and the Environment*, **1**, 351–8.

## Hurricanes

Brokaw, N.V.L. and Walker, L.R. (1991). Summary of the effects of Caribbean hurricanes on vegetation. *Biotropica*, **23**, 442–7.

Finkl, C.W. and Pilkey, O.H., eds. (1991). Impacts of Hurricane Hugo: September 10–22, 1989. *Journal of Coastal Research*, Special Issue No. 8.

Flannery, T. (2005). *The Weather Makers: How Man is Changing the Climate and What it Means for Life on Earth*. New York: Atlantic Monthly Press.

Walker, L.R. (2000). Seedling and sapling dynamics in treefall pits in Puerto Rico. *Biotropica*, **32**, 267–75.

Walker, L.R., Lodge, D.J., Brokaw, N.V.L. and Waide, R.B. (1991). An introduction to hurricanes in the Caribbean. *Biotropica*, **23**, 313–6.

Webb, S.L. (1999). Disturbance by wind in temperate-zone forests. In *Ecosystems of Disturbed Ground, Ecosystems of the World 16*, ed. L.R. Walker. Amsterdam: Elsevier, pp. 197–222.

Whigham, D.F., Dickinson, M.B. and Brokaw, N.V.L. (1999). Background canopy gap and catastrophic wind disturbances in tropical forests. In *Ecosystems of Disturbed Ground*, ed. L.R. Walker. Amsterdam: Elsevier, pp. 223–52.

Zaman, M.W. (1999). Vulnerability, disaster, and survival in Bangladesh: three case studies. In *The Angry Earth*, eds. A. Oliver-Smith and S.M. Hoffman. New York: Routledge, pp. 192–212.

Zimmerman, J.K., Willig, M.R., Walker, L.R. and Silver, W.L. (1996). Introduction: disturbance and Caribbean ecosystems. *Biotropica*, **28**, 414–23.


## Grazing

Crosby, A.W. (2004). *Ecological Imperialism: the Biological Expansion of Europe, 900–1900*. Cambridge: Cambridge University Press.

Low, T. (2001). *Feral Future: The Untold Story of Australia's Exotic Invaders*. Ringwood, Victoria, Australia: Penguin Books Australia, Ltd.

Mann, C.C. (2005). *1491: New Revelations of the Americas before Columbus*. New York: Alfred A. Knopf.

Miller, G.H., Fogel, M.L., Magee, J.W., Gagan, M.K., Clarke, S.J. and Johnson, B.J. (2005). Ecosystem collapse in Pleistocene Australia and a human role in megafaunal extinction. *Science*, **309**, 287–90.

# 7

## The lessons learned

### 7.1 INTRODUCTION

The earth has provided many lessons for humanity in the form of how to repair damage from natural disasters. Landscapes formed by natural calamities provide a theater for evolution (e.g. endemism on dunes and volcanoes, biodiversity enhancements following fires and variable landscapes created by glaciers, floods and landslides). These natural disasters are part of the environment, but their effects are ephemeral in the grand scheme of things ... ecosystems do recover. However, natural processes are often slow, leaving unproductive land that causes long-term privations, and a return to the previous *status quo* is never certain. We no longer have the luxury to wait for a natural recovery that, if it comes at all, will not produce welcome results. We face huge problems that challenge our ability to cope with complex, interacting systems. Social, political and economic problems are intensified by damage and destruction of the natural systems that support human populations. Addressing problems of resource supply and habitat restoration by applying lessons provided by natural recovery will improve our collective well-being and effectively promote security.

### 7.2 NATURE RECOVERS

Natural disturbances are an integral part of the physical and biological processes on Earth, and natural recovery ensures the continued health of the planet. Long before humans arrived, species evolved in the context of a constantly changing environment. The rich variety of plants, animals and microbes is a direct result of disturbance, followed by multiple patterns of evolution, each leading to a unique, successful way to cope with the environmental changes. Across broad areas of similar climate and disturbance regime, certain suites of organisms were consistently successful, leading to today's biomes (e.g. boreal forest, tropical forest, savanna, desert). Under the most severe disturbance regimes, few species survived, yet dispersal from the surroundings soon repopulated even surfaces such as freshly cooled lava. Nature recovered even after dramatic climatic fluctuations caused by ice ages or meteorite impacts that also caused the extinction of many species and altered the course of evolution. Humans have now fundamentally altered this recovery process.

### 7.3   HUMANS INTENSIFY DISTURBANCES

The Egyptians built their persistent, great empires on hard-won expertise in water management. Other societies, such as the Moche River people in sixth-century Peru, also produced intelligent and effective water management systems. Yet this Peruvian society disintegrated by AD 800. Brian Fagan eloquently discussed how despite effective means to cope with drought, the Moche River people could not overcome the triple impacts of drought, anchovy collapse and subsequent torrential floods, all events related to an extreme El Niño event. As their society weakened, stronger, more flexible and luckier neighbors overran them by the start of the ninth century. Any society can cope with some stress, but often it fails when suffering multiple stresses, or when bad choices are made.

While abrupt natural disasters such as volcanoes or floods are properly considered catastrophes, we have seen that humans intensify either the consequences of these events or they intensify the disaster itself. Humans tend to not notice long-term changes until it is too late. Salinization, overgrazing, erosion and invasion of exotic plants all slowly reduce the productivity of the land.

### 7.4   HOW HUMANITY ALTERS THE EQUATION

Humans have altered the earth in so many obvious ways, including mining, road building, agriculture and urbanization. More subtle alterations include a stunning increase in the background rate of species extinction, disruption of many complex food webs (e.g. by killing top predators such as cougars which cause plagues of herbivores and deforestation), massive rearrangement of the biota and our emerging role in global climate change. Essentially, the earth is now a mix of natural and anthropogenic forces, with the latter becoming ascendant.

We still cannot influence volcanism, earthquakes or tsunamis, but we do cause landslides, floods and fires. We have altered even hurricane intensity by increasing the temperature of tropical oceans. Our lives, initially intertwined with only natural disturbances, have become totally influenced by a new, worldwide disturbance regime that is part natural and part anthropogenic.

With our global dominance and alteration of most biological and some climatological and geological forces, we, and all other species, face a new game of survival. The rules have changed but we have yet to learn how they have changed and how to respond. In fact, they continue to change, as streams become polluted with hormones, the ground is polluted by excessive nitrogen deposition and the air receives all manner of other novel contaminants. The capacity for Nature to recover is altered by extinctions and habitat disruption. Our croplands replace many fertile, once diverse habitats with monocultures. Our honeybees alter what is pollinated, our markets what is dispersed. We need to find new paradigms to respond to this increasingly disrupted and biologically chaotic world.

Added to this grim image of increasing environmental stress is the realization that the effects are further intensified as the human populations increase in density and expand geographically. Fragmentation and invasive species have upset the mechanisms by which systems once recovered, and direct intervention to replace dispersal and control unwanted species appears to be the sole remaining option (see Fig. 1.3).

Success in the game of survival is definitely rooted in flexibility and responsiveness to changing conditions. Human ingenuity has led us from simple cave dwellers to technological geniuses. Yet sometimes we seem to forget the basic natural processes that we rely on to provide us with such primary resources as abundant water, fertile soil and clean air. Social, political and economic problems are intensified by damage to natural systems that support human populations. Without ready access to natural resources, societies historically have attempted to obtain resources by force. To the extent that habitats are restored to production, the impetus for war is reduced. Ecological rather than national security, through biological restoration, is urgently needed and will give us the best chance for long-term political and economic stability.

Repairing natural systems effectively and rapidly should become a major global priority. Yet, because all the ground rules have changed, we now have a different set of resources available. Human-altered landscapes are increasingly fragmented and filling with new mixes of agricultural, native and invasive species. Novel soil organisms, such as introduced earthworms, are altering decomposition and nutrient cycling. Such changes require new approaches to restoration. To develop such approaches we first have to learn from what remains of the processes of natural recovery, then modify them accordingly.

## 7.5   NATURAL MODELS PROVIDE LESSONS

We have learned that acid or toxic sites (e.g. mine or dredge spoils) can be reclaimed by ameliorating surfaces, creating safe-sites, altering fertility and introducing species tolerant of the adverse conditions. Landfills may be reclaimed by using bioremediation in early stages and by using species tolerant of drought. Creating safe-sites will enhance early growth. In most cases, the appropriate species need to be introduced and maintained because no suitable species can naturally encounter the site. The effectiveness of each of these solutions has been enhanced by a combination of empirical and theoretical lessons from successional studies.

## 7.6   BUT THE RULES HAVE CHANGED

While nature provides lessons about rules of a game that was once played, we have created a different game. The application of these lessons should be tempered and fit to the new reality. Increasingly, natural succession must be supplemented with ecological restoration to improve landscape diversity and stability. For instance, if you allocate a clearing within a city to a new urban park and just let it colonize naturally, you will get a novel set of plants and animals. Initially, weeds and ornamentals from other parks, roadways or backyards will invade and rats, mice, pigeons and other city animals will encroach. Eventually the park may get some plants from natural areas beyond the city or a few visits from migrating birds bringing native plant species. However, with no constructive intervention, the imprint of casual human actions on the park will always be great and persistent.

Ecological restoration improves the land by increasing biodiversity, promoting landform stability and enhancing the rate of recovery. By learning about and applying lessons from natural recovery processes, we can tailor our responses to the newly developing conditions. Only in that way can we improve the success of our efforts to rehabilitate devastated landscapes.

Infertile, unstable surfaces such as non-lava volcanic surfaces, dunes and glacial moraines are perhaps the most difficult surfaces to restore. Likewise, their analogs (e.g. mine tailings, gravel roads, landfills) present major hurdles to restoration. Stabilization to reduce erosion and permit plant establishment, particularly on dunes and mine tailings, is the first requirement for these surfaces. Dispersal can be promoted by attracting birds with perches or, better, by direct plantings, especially when the disturbed area is large. A few strategically placed trees not only attract dispersers, but also protect seedlings.

Drought on unstable surfaces can only be overcome as organic matter builds up to retain surface moisture. Nutrient additions are best, through planting nitrogen-fixing species rather than commercial fertilizers, to avoid arresting succession with dense swards of vegetation. Fertility can accelerate rates of succession in many cases, but competitive forces that inhibit development must necessarily be controlled. Careful monitoring of the balance between positive (facilitative) and negative (inhibitory) species interactions helps to ensure success. Restoration goals that emphasize establishment of ecological functions will be more successful targeting a pre-determined, arbitrary species mix. Yet even establishing partial vegetative cover can be difficult and time-consuming because of the twin challenges of infertility and instability on these substrates.

Infertile, stable surfaces such as lava or vertical cliff faces are also difficult to restore. Natural succession is particularly slow when there are no safe-sites for seedlings to establish. Cracks are very important as sites for the accumulation of debris and development of soil and any additions of fertilizer, such as from bird droppings, can improve plant growth. Stable, long-lived species that can tap moisture and nutrients in deep cracks and withstand periodic drought or erosion often dominate. These problems are faced by those restoring paved or heavily compacted roads, urban lots, mine pits, walls, road banks and other heavily compacted or sealed surfaces. Natural succession shows us that breaking up the surface is the first priority, in order to provide safe-sites for germination. Introduction of species, ideally by transplanting directly into these safe-sites, is also helpful. These introductions often will need to be maintained until well established. Exclusion of herbivores might also be necessary as new, palatable additions to a barren landscape are particularly vulnerable. Overall cover will likely remain low and recovery of ecosystem processes slow in such habitats, but there is much flexibility to create the desired community.

Fertile, unstable habitats such as landslides and low-energy land-water margins (floodplains, lakeshores, salt marshes and mangrove swamps) can easily be restored but may be disrupted frequently by recurring disturbance. Landslides are often of human origin yet native plants, often with vegetative reproduction, dominate. Ecological efforts are usually superior to imported plants or engineering solutions. Ultimately, slopes that are destabilized will continue to erode and humans forget that at their peril. Floodplain restoration should account for the seasonal fluctuations in water levels but can then proceed to many different endpoints. Floodplains and other shorelines are very susceptible to invasive species because of the fertility and readily available water, so restoration activities are now addressing many novel species interactions.

Fertile, stable habitats such as those impacted by fire, hurricane or grazing are relatively easy to restore so competition among colonizing plants has to be regulated. Competition begins with dispersal and goes through all subsequent stages of succession. Sometimes the first species to arrive in quantity dominates for a long time because it usurps resources from other potential colonizers. Vegetative reproduction from species surviving *in situ* can also aid restoration of pre-disturbance communities and help resist undesirable invasive species.

### 7.8   GUIDE TO REHABILITATION

For successful restoration to occur, several roadblocks must be overcome and the model of succession guides the strategies for success. Here we present a rough guide for achieving success in a small-scale restoration project (Fig. 7.1).

A preliminary assessment of soils, existing species, possible toxicity, residual habitat, biotic diversity and stresses will inform limitations and opportunities for the course to be followed (Fig. 7.1A). If possible, pilot studies should be conducted to refine estimates based on qualitative assessments, determine growth potential, test suitable species and determine needs for amelioration (Fig. 7.1B). During early site assessment and pilot programs, factors that could cause the restoration to fail should be noted, and taken into account during planning (Fig. 7.1C). At the Lehigh Gap restoration project (Box 7.1), it was essential to find the species that would grow before they were planted across the project.

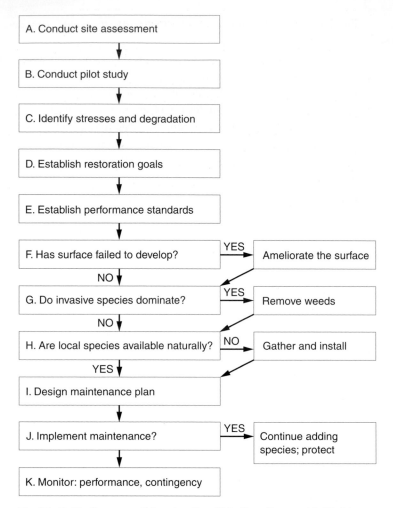

Fig. 7.1 Guide for successful restoration. This flow diagram highlights dangers that must be overcome to achieve success in small-scale restoration projects. (Modified from the following sources: Hobbs, 1999; Holms, 1999; Tordoff, Baker & Willis, 2000.)

Rehabilitation goals are, of course, based on proposed uses of the site, fiscal and labor constraints and social factors. However, the constraints of the site itself must be incorporated into these goals (Fig. 7.1D). The goals must be stated so that progress can be monitored during the project and quantified performance standards must be established (Fig. 7.1E).

The site may require amelioration before the introduction of any plants, particularly plants that have not naturally invaded (Fig. 7.1F).

Box 7.1  The Lehigh Gap Restoration Project

Lehigh Gap is a deep incision cut through Kittatinny Ridge by the
Lehigh River (Pennsylvania). A century ago, two zinc smelters began
operation. Coal fuel gave off sulfur dioxide and heavy metals,
including zinc, cadmium and lead, from the ore added to the toxic
brew that fell on the landscape. The vegetation throughout the
region was destroyed, leading to erosion of 0.5 m of rich soil and a
virtual desert. By 1980, the top 20 cm of soil was contaminated by
heavy metals and in 1983, the region became a Superfund site.
Natural recovery was recalcitrant, but under the guidance of Daniel
Kunkle, the nonprofit Wildlife Information Center was founded
in 2002 to shepherd the recovery on a 3 km² site, an exercise in
accelerated primary succession. Based on studies of post-glacial
succession and invasion on serpentine soils, warm season grasses
were selected to be the pioneers. Still in the early stages, the grasses
are building soil, and facilitating the eventual return of the
hardwood forest, but already provide welcome habitat diversity
reminiscent of pre-colonial times when Native Americans burned
forests to augment hunting. Plans call for the addition of more
herbs and small trees and the control of notorious woody plant
invaders. After five years, progress has exceeded even optimistic
expectations (Plate 15). At least ten species of grasses, planted after
physical amelioration of the site, are flourishing. The Center has
created a thriving community with functional decomposers and
a complex food web capped by foxes, coyotes and hawks. Long-term
management remains a key issue. Fire and the introduction of
additional species will challenge the managers. The methods are
being considered for application in other regional sites that mimic
primary succession. This project demonstrates how much can be
done with even limited resources. The site is becoming an amenity
for the surrounding villages.

Natural succession can only occur with those species that manage to
reach a site, a condition rarely encountered in urban or industrial
situations. However, if weeds have invaded, steps to control them are
crucial. Often a project fails because natural dispersal brings in swarms
of undesirable species. Their continued presence compromises most
projects (Fig. 7.1G). It is crucial that species introduced intentionally be
those appropriate to the goals. Introduced species can be those typical of
later stages of natural succession, so that managed succession can be

accelerated (Fig. 7.1H). However, projects also fail because too great a dependence is placed on natural dispersal, and little attention is paid to planting or seeding during the project.

A successful project depends on a long-term plan to maintain the site. Monitoring is used to compare the results to the performance standards and to determine if contingency plans are to be implemented (Fig. 7.1I; Plate 15). Frequently overlooked, but in accordance with natural succession, is the observation that small-scale secondary disturbances should be implemented to facilitate growth, to promote the natural invasion of desirable species or to promote a mosaic of vegetation. This may require a detailed maintenance plan and the addition of species at several stages during the project (Fig. 7.1J). Finally, monitoring must be a part of the plan in order to assess the progress and obtain early indications of problems associated with grazing, infertility, drought or other factors that could cause the project to fail.

This plan provides several stages for correcting problems before they become catastrophic. The process works best when the goals are clearly developed early in the process and those directly involved in the outcome can contribute to developing these goals. This strategy was adopted at Golden Gate National Park (San Francisco, California). In planning for restoration of dunes (Plate 16) and a salt marsh at Crissy Field, a former military airfield, local citizens and native people whose ancestors had lived on the spot were among those consulted.

### 7.9    A PLEA FOR BIODIVERSITY

In this book, we have argued from a largely utilitarian perspective. Enhanced restoration is desirable because it leads to greater goods and services for a human population already pressed against its biological limits. The long-term well-being of our species is tied directly to that of the rest of the biota. Fragmentation, climatic change, biological invasions and habitat destruction have already eliminated many species. Habitats throughout the world are being converted to human use at such an accelerated pace that just saving the remnants will not be enough to maintain biodiversity. Conservation needs to be wed to restoration if we expect to avoid catastrophic levels of species extinction.

The loss of biodiversity is a major threat to the economic security of all nations. Without secure access to natural resources found in efficient, productive settings, societies historically have attempted to obtain resources by force. To the extent that habitats are restored to production efficiently, an impetus for war is reduced. Habitat restoration can apply to large, formerly pristine areas as well as to small, heavily impacted sites. By attending to less traditional sites, such as remnants in urban areas or industrial sites, local people benefit, and pressures to exploit more land are reduced. Just as paper recycling reduces the demand for trees and conserves energy, recycling land has multiple benefits. For example, if recycled land is closer to the main population center than virgin land, the costs of transportation and the development of new infrastructures will be substantially lower. It will be less expensive to construct because a local workforce will be available, and other economies are likely to be possible.

Increasingly, it is not possible to find a semblance of natural vegetation. International commerce and tourism have accelerated the pace at which exotic species spread and invade even pristine habitats. On Hawaii, the nitrogen-fixing fire tree (*Myrica faya*) was introduced for ornamental purposes from the Azores, Canary Islands and Madeira. Then it was planted during the 1920s to reclaim watersheds, and now it is found throughout lava fields in the Hawaiian Volcanoes National Park, where it has reduced populations of the native tree called ōhià (*Metrosideros*). Conversely, the flora of the Canary Islands has been decimated by European weeds and by sugarcane. Perhaps the most desperate case is that of the small island of Réunion in the western Indian Ocean. The Piton de la Fournaise volcano is very active, creating new lavas, but only introduced species colonize these lavas.

### 7.10   THE FUTURE

We envision at least three mutually non-exclusive scenarios for humanity. First, humans have immense ingenuity to solve problems, especially when our survival is at stake and our attention is concentrated. If we can remove the blinders about our impact on the planet and apply our creative forces to the maintenance and accessibility of basic natural resources for everyone, there is hope for humanity. Yet, each *technological* fix produces new problems (dams lead to death of native fish, cars lead to air pollution, wind turbines impinge on bird flyways). Nonetheless, there are those who argue that technology, which got us to the current situation, remains our principal road to survival.

A second approach suggests that humans should gain control of their reproduction and reduce their material demands on the planet through conservation. This route is also difficult because it relies on a self-discipline that is rarely apparent. Progress is being achieved in the global reduction of poverty and disease; with improved living conditions and better education, birth rates generally do fall. However, increased wealth also leads to increased consumption and resource abuse. The most likely cultural paradigm to succeed will be, we believe, one that merges traditional emphasis on simple living and local food production with the modern benefits of health care and global communications.

A third scenario that we have explored in this book is to educate ourselves about habitat restoration to minimize damage and maximize productivity of the land. This approach also benefits from better understanding the processes of disturbance and how humans respond. How we interact with both natural and anthropogenic disturbances shapes our resource base, our resource use and our attitudes toward both technology and controlled growth. Our very sense of personal, national and global security rides on our relationship with natural resources (Can I afford to fill my car with gasoline? Should my country guarantee that possibility, even if it means going to war?)

We are optimistic that civilization as well as humanity will survive. Sustaining a progressive civilization will take technological tools, reduced population growth and improved responses to the disturbances that affect our resources and habitats. We must pay attention to the forces that led to the collapse of past civilizations and to the warning signs. Civilizations have tended to collapse when they were weakened by an abuse of natural resources, even though wars or pandemics may have triggered the collapse. Today, however, it is the whole globe, not just isolated civilizations, that must struggle to find an appropriate response to our challenges.

BIBLIOGRAPHY

Berry, W. (1977). *The Unsettling of America: Culture & Agriculture*. New York: Avon Books.

Bradshaw, A. D. and Chadwick, M. J. (1980). *The Restoration of the Land*. Berkeley: University of California Press.

Brown, L. R. (2006). *Plan B 2.0: Rescuing a Planet Under Stress and a Civilization in Trouble*. New York: W. W. Norton & Co.

Eldredge, N. (1998). *Life in the Balance*. Princeton, NJ: Princeton University Press.

Hobbs, R. J. (1999). Restoration of disturbed systems. In *Ecosystems of Disturbed Ground*, ed. L. R. Walker. Amsterdam: Elsevier, pp. 676–87.

Holms, P. M. and Richardson, D. M. (1999). Protocols for restoration based on recruitment dynamics. *Restoration Ecology*, **7**, 215–30.

Laurie, I. C., ed. (1979). *Nature in Cities*. New York: John Wiley & Sons.

Tordoff, G. M., Baker, A. J. M. and Willis, A. J. (2000). Current approaches to the revegetation and reclamation of metalliferous mine wastes. *Chemosphere*, **41**, 219–28.

# Glossary

| TERMS | DEFINITIONS |
|---|---|
| a'a lava | From Hawaiian for "stony rough lava", it has a rough, rubble surface composed of broken, loose and sharp fragments |
| abiotic | Pertaining to non-biological factors such as wind, temperature or erosion |
| AD | *Anno Domini*, literally "year of the (Christian) lord"; year since the accepted date of the birth of Jesus. Also called "Christian era" |
| aerenchyma | Any plant tissue with large, air-filled cavities |
| aerobic | Occurring in the presence of oxygen |
| alien species | A species from another region; non-native organism (see exotic species) |
| allelopathy | A form of inhibition based on the release of chemicals |
| alpha diversity | Changes in the number and distribution of species within a community |
| alternative steady states | Stable vegetation that results from a common origin |
| alvar | Flat, open area with shallow soil over calcareous bedrock |
| amelioration | Physical processes that reduce environmental stresses |
| anaerobic | Occurring in the absence of oxygen |
| anthropogenic | Caused by humans |
| assembly rules | Predictions concerning mechanisms of community organization |
| bandicoot | A rabbit-like marsupial from Australia |

| | |
|---|---|
| BC | Date in years before the Christian era (see AD); used for dates related to human events |
| beta diversity | Changes in the number and distribution of species along environmental (and temporal) gradients |
| biodiversity | Number and distribution of species; a measure of overall species richness |
| biogeography | Study of the distribution of organisms |
| biome | A geographical region with similar vegetation and climate (e.g. tropical forest, tundra – see also taiga) |
| bioremediation | Reclamation based on the use of plants to reduce toxicity |
| biotic | Pertaining to biological factors |
| bog | A wetland with low pH, usually saturated soil and dominance by mosses |
| boreal | See taiga |
| BP | Before the present, used for long, pre-historic dates. |
| browsing | Herbivory by vertebrates on leaves and stems of woody species |
| calcareous | Calcium-rich |
| cation exchange capacity | The ability of a soil to attract and hold such cations as potassium and ammonium |
| chaparral | Term used for dense shrub land adapted to frequent fires in Chile and the American Southwest; also called mallee (Australia), maquis (Mediterranean Europe), fynbos (South Africa) |
| chronosequence | A series of communities arrayed on the landscape presumed to represent a successional sequence (a space-for-time substitution) |
| chute | The path taken by landslides and avalanches |
| climax vegetation | Vegetation that has reached a stable state |
| colonization | The process of arrival and establishment in a new habitat |
| commons | Originally, a grazing land owned by all in common, but the animals owned by individuals |
| competition | The negative influence of one species on another due to sharing of limited resources |
| conflagration | An intense wildfire |

| | |
|---|---|
| coulee | Long, narrow spillway from a glacial lake |
| cryptogamic crust | A biotic crust on the soil surface composed of mosses, lichens, algae and liverworts |
| debris avalanche | A wet landslide consisting of more solid material than water (see lahar) |
| deflected succession | Succession that is altered from its normal course by disturbance |
| degradation | Any process that reduces the biodiversity, productivity or other desirable trait of an ecosystem |
| derelict sites | Habitats that have been severely degraded, usually in an urban setting |
| desalinization | Reduction of salt levels at a site using physical or biotic processes |
| desertification | The conversion of range land to desert with low value |
| dispersal | The process by which an organism or its reproductive units are transferred from their place of origin to another location |
| disturbance | A relatively discrete event in time and space that alters habitat structure and often involves a loss of biomass |
| disturbance intensity | The physical force of a disturbance |
| disturbance regime | The composite influence of all disturbances at a particular site |
| disturbance severity | The degree to which a disturbance damages the biota |
| dormancy | A resting stage, often associated with seeds, but also with bulbs |
| dune slack | The protected, relatively stable and often moist habitat inland from the leading coastal dune |
| ecosystem | The sum of all organisms within a well-defined area, the physical environment and the interactions between them |
| ecosystem function | Process that defines the workings of an ecosystem, such as nutrient dynamics |
| ecosystem service | Seen from a human perspective, such products as clean water and wildlife habitat. |
| ecosystem structure | Physical aspects of an ecosystem such as biomass, diversity and plant cover |

| | |
|---|---|
| ecotypes | Populations of a species that differ morphologically or physiologically |
| edaphic | Pertaining to soils |
| eutrophication | The process by which an aquatic system becomes more fertile; usually a negative result ensues |
| evapotranspiration | Water loss from an ecosystem due to transpiration from plants and evaporation from soil and water surfaces |
| exotic species | Species not native to the location; often a weed (see alien species) |
| extinction | The loss of a species from the system under study |
| facilitation | The positive influence of one species on another in a successional context |
| feedback loop | Situation where two or more factors interact to mutually affect their status |
| fen | An oligotrophic, acidic habitat dominated by herbaceous species, not mosses; frequently saturated with water |
| forb | Any herbaceous species excluding grasses |
| fragmentation | The biogeographic process of dividing a landscape, as through urbanization |
| fuel load | The amount of combustible material in vegetation |
| functional group | Species that share physiological, morphological or behavioral traits |
| fynbos | South African variant of chaparral, from Afrikaans for "fine bush" which describes many species that have narrow, fine, needle-like leaves |
| gabion | A structure, usually made of rock, designed to retain slopes and minimize landslides |
| gallery forest | The forests that occur along riparian corridors, especially in rainforests |
| gamma diversity | Changes in the number and distribution of species across landscapes |
| glacial foreland | The terrain exposed by a receding (melting) glacier |
| glacial moraine | The debris deposited by the retreat of a glacier |
| global warming | The gradual increase in the earth's temperature due largely to human activities |
| grazing | Herbivory on grasses and other herbs |
| greywacke | A variety of sandstone with many rock fragments embedded in a clay matrix |

| | |
|---|---|
| guano | An accumulation of sea bird droppings rich in phosphates and nitrates |
| habitat heterogeneity | Diversity of habitats within an ecosystem |
| herbivore | An organism that eats plant parts |
| herbivory | The consumption of all or part of living plants |
| inhibition | Any mechanism by which one species reduces the success of another (see inhibition model) in a successional context |
| initial floristic composition | Egler's hypothesis that trajectories are determined from the species inhabiting a site immediately after the disturbance |
| *jökulhlaup* | Massive flood resulting from the rupture of a glacial ice dam |
| karst | Irregular limestone terrain often dissected by caves, sinks and subterraneen streams |
| keystone species | Species that are crucial to the development or maintenance of a system |
| lahar | A slurry of mud and debris normally created by rapidly melting ice during a volcanic eruption |
| landscape ecology | The study of interactions of physical and biological phenomena across large regions |
| *lapilli* | Rounded to angular stone fragments |
| lenticel | Small spot on stems where roots may protrude |
| life history characteristics | The species-specific patterns of arrival, growth and longevity |
| loess | A fine, unconsolidated, wind-blown sediment |
| macroclimate | The climate of a large region |
| mangrove | Subtropical and tropical woodland that occupies shallow tidal ecosystems |
| marsh | Any wetland dominated by herbaceous species |
| mature ecosystem | A well developed ecosystem in which the rate of biomass accumulation and of species turnover are slow |
| microclimate | The climate directly experienced by an organism |
| microtopography | Small-scale physical features of the land such as furrows or ridges |
| microsite | Small scale habitat (see safe-sites) |
| mine tailings | The wastes remaining after extraction of minerals or fossil fuels |

| | |
|---|---|
| monadnock | An isolated hill or mountain surrounded by less resistant rock |
| monitoring | The record of the progress of biological and physical features during a rehabilitation project |
| mosaic | A patchwork of vegetation that results from small disturbances, differential succession rates or other factors |
| mutualism | A biotic interaction among different species that is beneficial to both |
| mycorrhizae | Fungi that form mutualistic interactions with higher plants |
| net primary productivity | The sum of all plant biomass generated in a given time and place |
| *nuée ardentes* | See pyroclastic flow |
| nunataks | Refugia that escaped glaciation |
| nurse plant | An established individual that alters its immediate surroundings in ways that favor the establishment of another plant |
| obsidian | Volcanic glass formed from rapid cooling of lava |
| organic matter | That portion of the soil derived from organisms |
| pahoehoe | From Hawaiian (for "smooth, unbroken lava"), it has a hummocky or ropy surface |
| pane | An impervious layer within a salt marsh that retains water |
| patch dynamics | The concept that the vegetation on a landscape is composed of groups of organisms at different stages of succession and is subject to different disturbance regimes |
| pathogen | A disease-producing organism |
| pedogenesis | The formation of soil |
| performance standards | That part of a rehabilitation project that specifies the parameters (e.g. survival, composition) that will define success |
| pioneer | A plant that colonizes a disturbed area, thereby initiating succession |
| pneumatophore | The air-breathing roots common to mangroves and other aquatic woody plants |
| podzol | A soil profile with extensive leaching of minerals to the lower B horizon |
| polder | A low-lying area reclaimed from the sea and |

protected by dikes

predation                a) The capture and consumption of one animal
                         by another; b) a form of herbivory in which
                         consumption results in the death of the target
                         (e.g. seed predation, herbivory on an annual
                         plant).

prescribed burn          A controlled fire designed to reduce the threat of
                         wildfire, rejuvenate the vegetation or reduce
                         exotic species

primary                  Production of plant biomass
    productivity

primary                  Ecosystem development and species change on
    succession           barren surfaces where severe disturbances
                         have removed most plants and soil

priority effects         The consequences of arrival order that condition
                         subsequent compositional changes

propagule                Any reproductive unit that is adapted to dispersal

pumice                   A silica-rich volcanic rock usually ejected during
                         explosive eruptions

pyroclastic flows        Volcanic material ejected at extreme temperatures
                         and which moves rapidly

pyrogenic                Refers to vegetation that is particularly flammable

quoll                    A small, carnivorous marsupial

reallocation             The conscious transformation of a landscape to a
                         condition or use distinct from its original one

reclamation              The conversion of wasteland to some productive
                         use by conscious intervention

refugia                  Isolated patches that escape a disturbance and
                         can initiate a succession (see relict species)

rehabilitation           Any manipulation of a sere to enhance its rate or to
                         deflect its trajectory toward a specified goal;
                         includes reclamation and restoration as two
                         extremes of intervention

rejuvenate               To reinvigorate vegetation, often through burn-
                         ing

relict species           A species surviving in a refuge within a large,
                         newly created landscape

resilience               The ability of an ecosystem to recover from
                         disturbance

restoration              Returning the land to its former biological status

return interval          The time between disturbance events at a

|   |   |
|---|---|
| | given site |
| rhizosphere | The soil around a root influenced by root activities such as exudates |
| rhyolite | A type of lava high in quartz and often grey to pink in color |
| riparian | Pertaining to growth along a stream corridor |
| rock outcrop | Bare rock surface undergoing primary succession |
| ruderal | A weedy plant that colonizes recent disturbances |
| safe-site | A microsite where seeds have an enhanced chance to lodge, germinate and establish |
| salinization | The process by which soil becomes increasingly saline |
| salt marsh | A coastal wetland characterized by tidal fluctuations, steep gradients and anoxic soils |
| *sandur* | Broad, sandy outwash plain formed by deposits of a massive lahar |
| scoria | A dense form of tephra that dominates many explosive volcanoes |
| secondary succession | Species change on habitats where soils remain relatively intact |
| seed bank | Dormant seeds found in the soil; often useful in rehabilitation |
| seed rain | The input of plant propagules onto a denuded site |
| sere | A term that denotes a stage in succession |
| shifting agriculture | Rotation among several fields, each used for a few years, then abandoned |
| silviculture | The scientific practice of growing trees efficiently |
| slash and burn | Conversion of forest to agricultural purposes, gradually moving across the landscape; leads to permanent conversion of forest to pasture |
| slip face | The exposed cliff revealed after an avalanche, mudflow or landslide |
| species turnover | A measure of succession, describing the sequential replacement of species through time |
| spontaneous succession | Succession that occurs without human intervention; usually weeds |
| stability | A community characteristic expressing a) the lack of change; b) resistance to disturbance |
| stabilization | The process by which vegetation of a sere ceases to change dramatically; other attributes may |

| | |
|---|---|
| | continue to develop |
| stolon | A horizontal stem that can produce new growth at its tip |
| stress | Any factor that limits the rate of productivity (e.g. infertility, drought, cold, heat, toxicity) |
| stump sprout | The rejuvenating remnant of a shrub or tree after a fire |
| succession | The process by which barren or damaged land recovers |
| succession rate | The rate of species replacement during succession |
| swamp | A wetland dominated by woody species |
| symbiont | A participant in a mutually beneficial link between two organisms |
| taiga | Cold forest dominated by conifers |
| talus | Piles of rocks fallen from a slope |
| target | The goal of a restoration project including the desired species composition |
| tectonic plate | A major component of the earth's crust that moves on the surface; some types of earthquakes occur when two plates collide |
| tephra | Any volcanic ejecta that is expelled into the air before falling to earth (see pumice and scoria) |
| *tepui* | Table-form sandstone mountains 400–2000 m above forests in Northern South America with many endemic species |
| threshold of irreversibility | The level of degradation below which an ecosystem is unlikely to recover without direct intervention |
| tolerance | The ability of a plant to persist despite adverse environmental conditions |
| tolerance model | A hypothesis that suggests that species replacements result from invasion (or persistence) of species more able to tolerate adverse environmental conditions |
| toposequence | A series of communities arrayed on the landscape in response to physical factors, not time |
| topsoil | The organically rich surface layer that often contains seeds and other regenerating organs |
| trajectory | The course traveled by vegetation from its |

|  | initiation to stability |
| accelerated | The rate of species replacement occurs more rapidly than normal due to management intervention |
| allogenic | The trajectory is controlled by external factors such as seed dispersal |
| arrested | The development of a sere is delayed in response to such factors as grazing dominance by one species, such as a thicket-former |
| autogenic | The trajectory is controlled by internal factors such as competition |
| convergent | a) a sere develops increasing similarity to a local community; b) two seres become increasingly similar to each other |
| deflected | A sere does not follow an expected trajectory due to management intervention or to the introduction of exotic species |
| deterministic | a) referring to models that always produce the same result; b) referring to the concept that a trajectory can be confidently predicted |
| divergent | Two seres develop decreasing similarity through time |
| parallel | Two seres neither converge nor diverge; each retains its relationship to its microsite |
| retrogressive | A sere develops reduced stature, biomass or diversity at odds with the prediction of progressive development; often due to erosion, mineral leaching or chronic disturbance; identical to regressive |
| stochastic | Referring to probabilistic transitions between seres; or to certain succession models |
| reticulate (network) | A set of trajectories that coalesce and diverge during succession |
| tidal bore | strong waves forced upstream in coastal rivers |
| tuya | Inuit, a flat-topped mountain formed when lava meets ice |
| vital attribute | A characteristic of a plant that determines the ways in which it can respond to major disturbance; e.g. the occurrence of seeds that persist on cones, fire stimulated seeds or |

buried regenerating organs

viviparity          Production on live offspring

wetland             Any habitat in which soils are saturated or
                    inundated for a significant time

xerarch sere        Succession that starts in a dry (xeric) habitat and
                    gets progressively wetter

zonation            A pattern of vegetation in response to a steep
                    environmental gradient that can be recog-
                    nized by the rapid replacement of the domi-
                    nant species

# Illustration Credits

Simon Baker (Manitou Springs, Colorado): Fig. 4.14.

Rowan Buxton (Landcare Research, New Zealand): Fig. 2.1.

Marcelino de la Cruz Rot (Universidad Politécnica de Madrid, Madrid, Spain): Fig. 5.2.

Roger del Moral: Figs. 1.2; 2.2; 3.1; 3.2; 3.3; 3.4; 3.5; 3.8; 3.9; 3.10; 3.11; 3.12; 3.13; 3.14; 3.15; 4.1; 4.4; 4.10; 4.11; 5.5; 5.15; 5.16; 6.1; 6.9; Plates 1; 4; 6; 7; 9; 11; 12; 16; Back Cover.

Willard E. Hayes, II (University of Nevada, Las Vegas): Fig. 5.13; Plate 10.

Shane Hona (Landcare Research, New Zealand): Fig. 5.14.

Dan Kunkle (Wildlife Information Center, Slatington, Pennsylvania): Plate 15.

Ariel Lugo (International Institute of Tropical Forestry, San Juan, Puerto Rico): Fig. 6.5; Plate 2.

Thomas Marler (University of Guam, Mangilao, Guam): Fig. 2.4.

David Mackenzie (CSIRO, Canberra): Fig. 6.2 A, B.

Elizabeth A. Powell (Boulder City, Nevada): Fig. 6.10.

Alan Trimble (University of Washington, Seattle): Fig. 5.18.

Lawrence Walker: Figs. 1.1; 1.4; 3.6; 3.7 A-F; 3.16; 3.17; 3.18; 3.19; 4.2; 4.3; 4.5; 4.6; 4.7; 4.8; 4.9; 4.13; 5.1; 5.3; 5.4 A-C; 5.6; 5.7; 5.8; 5.9; 5.10; 5.11; 5.12; 5.17; 6.3; 6.4; 6.6; 6.7; 6.8; Plates 3; 5; 8; 13; 14; Front Cover.

# Index